D1084205

THE WORLD OF THE ELSEVIERS
1580–1712

THE WORLD OF
THE ELSEVIERS
1580 - 1712

DAVID W. DAVIES

1954
MARTINUS NIJHOFF
THE HAGUE

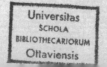

Composed in Monotype Baskerville
N.V. van de Garde & Co's Drukkerij, Zaltbommel
Typography H. van Krimpen
Printed in the Netherlands

Preface

IN the following pages an attempt has been made to give the essential facts of the history of the Elsevier family, and to show the relations of the printers to the world around them. Printing and publishing history is sometimes written as personal reminiscence, as aesthetic or technical criticism, or as a guide for book collectors. There is something to be said for treating it as a phase of economic or social history, and this treatment has been attempted here. There are difficulties inherent in the task which are not at first apparent. Printers are in touch on the one hand with the world of manufacturing and commerce, and on the other hand with the world of literature and scholarship – with not merely one phase of literature and learning but with a great many. As a result the innocent enthusiast who attempts to follow the activities of a publisher as he moves in the various milieux will constantly find himself in strange regions he knows nothing about. He will probably wish he had never entered them, and his learned readers will probably wish so, too.

So much assistance from friends has been sought and given that the story presented is a mosaic of the learning of others. The writer has reserved for himself only the special province of errors and omissions, and hereby lays claim to all such as may be found. It is a pleasant task to list those who have given information and assistance at various times: Professor Dr P. GEYL, University of Utrecht; Dr A. KESSEN, University of Leyden; Notaris H. A. WARMELINK, Amsterdam; Mr WILLEM SWETS and Miss ANNA

Swets, Hilversum; Miss Sarah Reed, University of
Chicago; Dr Benjamin Bart, University of Michigan;
Dr Philip Merlan, Scripps College; Mr Lyle Wright,
Huntington Library; Miss Thea Verboom, Claremont
College Library.

Special acknowledgment is made to the International
University Foundation and to Professor J. Anton de
Haas, who made it possible for the writer to work for
some time in the Netherlands.

The spelling 'Elsevier' has been adopted since that
seems to have been most common in the seventeenth
century. The spelling 'Leyden' has been used since that is
perhaps more familiar to English readers.

Claremont   David W. Davies
December, 1953

Contents

I

The First of the Elseviers

THERE are difficulties in tracing the history of a printer not encountered in following the career of kings or statesmen. The printer is not praised by courtly chroniclers, or slandered by troublesome democrats. His activities are dimly glimpsed in baptismal and marriage registers, in commercial and legal records. From such sources it has been learned that Louis Elsevier, the first of the name to achieve fame as publisher and bookseller, was born at Louvain (where his ancestors had lived for centuries) in 1546 or 1547, the son of 'Hans of Louvain,' a printer. All known facts of his early life are derived from similar barren entries in official records. A narrative based on such data has the verve and suspense of a telephone directory. It is only when the facts are viewed in conjunction with the course of history in general that they possess vitality and interest. The bare bones of Louis Elsevier's story, for example, the facts that he was Protestant and a bookbinder, that he migrated from Louvain to Antwerp, to Liège, to Douai, to Leyden, have interest and meaning only when added to knowledge of the Protestants in the Netherlands, the attitude of journeymen generally toward politics, the history of Netherlands cities. It will be of some service to the reader to gather the data which give meaning to Elsevier history.

I

Concerning the city of that 'Hans of Louvain called Helsevire,' the father of the hero of the piece, some points are of interest. In the Middle Ages Louvain had been the center of the Netherlands woolen trade, but its commercial prosperity had declined by the sixteenth century. By that time it was noted not for commerce but for its University. When Hans of Louvain took up his trade in the town, the University was still a glorious one, having six thousand students and many illustrious professors. It was the center of humanist letters, between 1490 and 1520 having numbered among its members the future Pope, Adrian VI, Erasmus, Van den Dorp, Luis Vives, Costers and de Palude. The place had filled Erasmus with delight. 'I do not know,' he wrote, 'if ever among any people good letters have been better established than here.' The University not only encouraged good letters but cultivated the art of printing, at one time having under its protection the 'Aldus of the Netherlands,' Thierry Martens, a fine scholar, a fine printer, and an editor of More's *Utopia*. The town was, then, a favorable location for a printer such as Hans Elsevier. Since his son, Louis, grew up in the milieu of printer's ink, on the fringe of academic society, the trade of bookbinder was a natural one for him to adopt.

No further facts are known about Louis until his marriage to Marie du Verdin (Mayke Duverdyn) which occurred in 1563 when Louis was about eighteen. Soon after (by 1565), both Louis and his father moved to Antwerp. The precise reasons for the migration cannot be fixed, but they can be guessed. In the opinion of many the University of Louvain by that date had passed its zenith; Erasmus, the apostle of good letters, and his famous contemporaries had been long dead. Antwerp, chief commercial city of the Netherlands, on the contrary, probably had its year of greatest prosperity in 1560. The city was the meeting place for Spanish and Portuguese merchants trading in the Mediterranean, the East Indies, and the Americas, for Germans, Zeelanders, and Hollanders trading with Baltic cities and Scandinavia. Within its precincts lived one hundred thousand people, including whole colonies of English, Spanish, Portuguese and German merchants. It was also the banking center of the world, and at its docks along the Scheldt sometimes as many as two hundred and fifty ships were unloading at one time. There was as much business transacted at Antwerp in a fortnight, the Venetian envoy wrote, as was transacted at Venice in a year.

The city had ample printing and publishing facilities; indeed, in the opinion of conservatives, facilities were too ample. Plantin was the most famous printer of the town, but other excellent printers, Willem Silvius, Nutius, Bellerus and Johann Steels, also worked there. Of the somewhat more than four thousand books appearing in the Netherlands between 1500 and 1540, two thousand two hundred and thirty were published at Antwerp. It is understandable that Louis Elsevier and his father should move to the large city. Having migrated, they wanted naturally to work in a good shop, and so both got jobs with Plantin. The name of the pressman, 'Hans of Louvain called Helsevire,' appears numerous times in the records of workmen employed at the Plantin house after 1565. The evidence of Louis Elsevier's connections with Plantin are not so numerous, but in the Plantin-Moretus Museum there is a large folio manuscript volume written in Plantin's hand entitled *Book of the Workmen employed by the Printing House*. For the year 1565 there are entries which read substantially as follows:

3

21 January, Loys Helsevire for 53 reams, gathered
    and collated   1.6½ florins
29 January, Louis Helsevire for 69 reams of *Les Secrets
    d'Alexis Piemontoys* and of the *Epistolae Ciceronis,*
    etc.   1.14½ florins
23 February to Louis Helsevire for 9 days   2   florins
 4 March, to Louis Helsevire for 6 days, at 4½ per day 1.7   florins
11 April, for having aided in parcelling up the Bible 0.3   florins

The connection thus formed with Plantin by Elsevier was probably never completely broken during the lifetime of the former. According to records in the Plantin archives, when Louis was living at Douai, in 1578 and 1579, he did work for his old employer; and later at Leyden, as will be evident, his connections with Plantin were many. Of Louis' days at Antwerp, one may conjure up a picture, not too erroneous, of an ambitious young journeyman bookbinder settled in the biggest city of an important country, employed by the best firm in town. His family was growing: Mathijs, the future university beadle, was born about 1565; and Louis, his second son, who later conducted a business at The Hague, was born in 1566. It does not appear from available records that young Louis Elsevier enjoyed an exalted position at the Plantin press. It appears that he was folding and collating signatures, and wrapping packages, but it is possible that he may have been entrusted with important work also. At any rate, he had secured a foothold in the city, and if it had not been for the reverberations of a few world-shaking events, he would have been what is known as a young man with good prospects.

There were political clouds on the horizon, and as a matter of fact, many of these clouds were bursting over Antwerp during the first years of Louis' stay in the city.

4

The Lowlands, in the years from 1560 to 1609, were in the midst of that famous sequence of events which is called 'the revolt of the Netherlands,' and there was a sea of trouble in Antwerp. There were economic as well as political and religious difficulties. The Antwerp financial men were bankers for the sovereigns of Europe, but even in 1560 the credit of the sovereign majesties of France, Spain and Portugal was exhausted; the royal gentlemen were no longer good for their debts. The effect on bankers was calamitous; one after another they went bankrupt. In the wake of the banking disaster, unemployment and hard times rippled over an ever-widening area. Protestantism was growing in the city by leaps and bounds; Louis Elsevier was himself converted to Protestantism at Antwerp. In a country ruled by a Spanish king considering himself the special protector of Catholicism, this heretical movement could result in nothing but trouble. Those of the reformed persuasion were largely laborers and small craftsmen, and as Antwerp prosperity faded they grew bitter and discontented; they became rebels at heart and, as one historian said, they had 'democracy in their blood.'

The printers of the city were especially objectionable. Good Catholics thought too much liberty was allowed them, that they all ought to be sent to Louvain, or Douai, where they could be better controlled. It was a scandal that one could buy books of Luther, Melanchthon, Zwingli, Calvin or Bucer at several printing offices in town. In 1559 more than a score of heretics were executed, in 1560 more than a score more, but it did no good. The dangerous situation created by Protestants was worsened by the great nobles who were antagonistic to the officials whom Philip of Spain placed over them. In 1566 the

Prince of Orange and his disaffected fellow aristocrats rode in and took command of Antwerp. Ostensibly their task was to maintain order, but the Protestants saw in them possible allies. The Calvinists were emboldened, embarked on an orgy of sacking Catholic churches, and an epidemic of desecration ran through the Netherlands. In the following year there was an armed rising, and this brought to the town the terrible Duke of Alva and his Spanish troops, bent on vengeance. As Alva came into the city many Protestants fled, among them Louis Elsevier and his family. It was the wise thing to do. In that year and the years immediately following many printers were banished or imprisoned for selling what were variously termed scandalous, evil, seditious, or Lutheran books. The printer Willem Silvius, who remained in Antwerp, was arrested and accused of taking part in the sacking of churches. Though nothing could be proved against him, his six-week sojourn in jail was enough to ruin his business. In 1572 a visitor wrote that the city of Antwerp was disappearing like melting snow.

Since the Netherlands' revolt, which sent Louis (and hundreds of others) scurrying to Liège, was to drive him to Wesel, to Douai, and finally to Leyden, there is profit in remembering the more obvious facts about the famous occurrence. The event has occupied the imagination and the energies of many historians and storytellers. When one looks for its causes one finds they were manifold. The Netherlanders (both those who spoke French and those who spoke Netherlandish) were ruled by the Spanish, an alien race. They were a commercial people imposed upon by a soldiery, and they were taxed to support a foreign government. The Netherlands Protestants, though a minority, were militantly anti-Catholic, which meant in

6

that day that they were anti-government. It was a war between those who loved the old medieval ways of particularism and privilege and those who held new ideas of centralization and absolutism. Patriotism, of course, was among the motives for rebellion, but it would be wrong to assume that the great lords who led the revolt, the Prince of Orange, Brederode, Egmont and Hoorn, had this as their only motive. Like their peers in other lands, they disputed kingship as an action fitting to them. They felt that while rebellion for a commoner was treason, rebellion for a noble had something in it of nobility, it being the duty of a lord to play a great part. These were some of the factors inducing rebellion, which broke with equal fury in north and south Netherlands, which went favorably first for one side and then for the other, and which ended with the independence of the northern provinces situated safely behind the rivers, and the subjection of the southern provinces which were on the wrong side of that strategic barrier. The final outcome, submission for the south, freedom for the north, began to take shape as early as 1572 when the 'Sea Beggars,' sea-going adherents of William of Orange, captured the town of Brielle, and aided William in the ensuing conquest of Holland and Zeeland provinces.

When Louis Elsevier, temporarily on the losing side at Antwerp, fled to Liège, his wife's native city, he probably made a wise choice of refuge. The bishopric of Liège was a Catholic but not a Spanish land, and in the year before Louis' arrival the reformed religion spread so rapidly there that for a time it appeared probable it would become the dominant one. Although this triumph of Calvinism in their country was short lived, the people of Liège, especially of the city of Liège, showed ardent sympathy

7

for the victims of the Duke of Alva. The sympathy did not spring entirely from generous hearts. The ruler of Liège, Bishop Groesbeek, was devoted to the Spanish cause; since the citizens of Liège suspected him of seeking to curtail their ancient liberties, they were against anything he was for, hence anti-Spanish. There was another reason why the city was a good place for exiles. Although in point of years a very old town, because of new collieries and rapidly increasing numbers of smiths and armorers, it had become a brisk manufacturing center. In this new era guilds and corporations lost much of their power. The status of tradesman was obtained with singular facility, accorded liberally to all who asked for it, strangers as well as natives. Thus, the records show that fleeing to Liège in 1567, Elsevier was admitted bookseller and citizen in 1569–70. In spite of painstaking search no further information on his activities at Liège has been found. In any event his stay there could not have been long, for between 1570 and 1574 he moved to Wesel. This ancient Hansa town, just outside the borders of the Netherlands in the Duchy of Cleves, had from the early years of the Reformation been a refuge for Netherlands Protestants. By 1568 Netherlands Calvinists in the city were so numerous that it seemed the logical place to hold a synod for the region, and the printing presses of the town poured forth books and pamphlets on the new doctrines. If, as it appears, Louis was by now bookseller as well as bookbinder, then Wesel was also a likely place for business.

But Louis' wanderings were far from over. At home in the Netherlands conditions were improving for Protestants like himself. The Duke of Alva had attempted to stamp out Protestantism with fire and sword, but after six years of effort it was not stamped out, and the effort was impoverishing Spain. In 1573 Alva was recalled and replaced by Don Luis de Requesens, who attempted to do by reasonableness and conciliation what Alva had failed to do by terror. In the name of Philip of Spain, Requesens issued a general pardon offering forgiveness to all erring subjects on condition they return to the church. It is evident Louis Elsevier took advantage of the pardon, but in returning to the Netherlands he went to Douai rather than to Antwerp. The year Elsevier returned, Antwerp had suffered the double calamity of plague and mutiny of the Spanish soldiers in which six thousand citizens were killed, whereas at Douai there was a new and promising university. It was modeled on Louvain and the majority of its first professors were from that University. For Elsevier, going to Douai meant returning to much that he had known; he may even have gotten back old customers! For a number of years to come conditions at Douai continued to improve for those of his persuasion. In 1576, for example, occurred the Pacification of Ghent. This was an agreement between Holland and Zeeland on the one hand, and Brabant, Flanders, and Hainaut on the other, to unite in the effort to rid the country of Spanish soldiers. The States General were to be called to settle the religious question and, until that time, the edicts against heretics were to be everywhere suspended.

Soon after this, in 1576, city governments came into power in many Netherlands cities which were hostile to Spain. As a result, many Flemings, Brabanters and Walloons returned from exile in Holland, Zeeland and England. By 1578 Ghent was virtually in Calvinist hands, and the resurgence of Calvinism was felt in Douai. When, in 1578, the Nobles and Clergy of the Estates of Artois proposed to conclude peace with Don Juan, the Spanish governor, there were disturbances in Douai, and in October of the same year Jesuits were expelled from the city. But the tide soon turned, and Louis was to resume his wanderings. On 6 January 1579 deputies of the Estates of Artois and Hainaut met at the Abbey of Saint Vaast with those of Douai and formed the Union of Arras, an agreement which made it evident that the Walloon, that is, French-speaking provinces, would submit to Spain and remain Catholic. We might assume that the turn of events was discerned by Elsevier. Toward the end of the year 1580 he gathered together his numerous family, his wife, his five sons, his daughter, his sister-in-law and her daughter, and migrated for the last time. This time he chose Leyden in the embattled province of Holland. He was but one of many émigrés to that province and to Zeeland, though certainly he was in an early wave of emigration. In 1585, for example, the single Calvinist community of Middelburg in Zeeland was enlarged by one thousand one hundred and fifty-five new members. The following year the Duke of Leicester authorized a hundred and thirty Walloon families, then refugees at Antwerp, to establish themselves in the northern provinces. At Ghent the report ran that nine thousand passports had been demanded after the city fell to the Spanish, and for a long time a third of the houses stood vacant in that city. The greater part of the Calvinists were literate bourgeoisie, merchants or highly skilled artisans. Their departure deprived South Netherlands of the more active and better educated elements and enriched the northern provinces. The names of immigrants are found in the forefront of many lines of endeavor. Frans van Aerssen, distinguished diplomat and curator of Leyden University, was from Brussels; Daniel Heinsius, one of the great scholars of his day, was from Ghent; Simon Stevin, who still has a place in the history of mathematics, was from Bruges, as was Gomarus, the antagonist of Arminius; the merchant Isaac Lemaire and his explorer son, Jacques, were from Tournay; Usselincx, the moving spirit of the Swedish settlement on the Delaware, was from Antwerp.

Elsevier arrived in Leyden when he was about thirty-three, not a bad age to seek a foothold in a strange city. He was courageous and likeable, and gained such a firm place that for more than a century and a quarter there were Elsevier printers and booksellers in the city. For more than a century the Elseviers were to have official connections with Leyden University. Their press grew famous, largely by publishing books needed in the University, or written by members of the University; and visitors sought out the establishment as a show place. Because of the long association of the press with town and University, it is helpful for those interested in Elseviers to remember the salient facts about the city and the famous academy.

The city had undergone, from May to October 1574, a terrible siege by the Spanish army, during which starvation and suffering were brought to the citizens. Some of those within the walls wished to surrender the place to the besiegers. A few iron-willed men held the town for the Prince until dykes were pierced, river water flowed up to the city walls, and Orange's sea beggars sailed in to break the siege. For the remainder of the war the city was dominated by patriots and fared well, since it had contact with oversea merchants, an advantage denied towns held by the Spanish. When Elsevier came to Leyden, not many years after the siege, it was a virile city with a great future, to become in the following century the greatest textile city of Europe. It impressed some and repelled others. Jean François Le Petit, in a translation of his work which appeared at London in 1609, said that Leyden was 'fairly seated in a delicate prospective, even in the heart of *Holland*, neatly built and fit for the muses to dwel in.' Scaliger, on the contrary, described it as a swamp within a swamp.

For the greater part of the seventeenth century Elseviers were to be printers to the University at Leyden, which had been founded in 1575, immediately following the siege, at the suggestion of the Prince of Orange. Within fifty years it became outstanding among the universities of Europe, and it was this institution which drew Louis Elsevier to the city, as it attracted other printers and booksellers. Willem Silvius, who had suffered for his religion at Antwerp, preceded Elsevier to Leyden, and Plantin and Ravelinghen followed him. Although modeled on Louvain, Leyden University was in several respects different from its model. It was a provincial university. Burgomasters and delegates of the States of Holland sat on its board of curators or trustees, making its governing body similar to those of modern state universities. It showed modernity and vitality in other ways. There was, for example, to be no discrimination for entrance on the grounds of religion. Calvinists, Lutherans, Jews, and even Catholics were to be received with equal hospitality. Universities in those days followed a traditional scheme of four faculties: law, medicine, theology, and philosophy; but Leyden was not long in adding to these such appendages of modern universities as an engineering school, botanic garden, observatory, and university press.

Originally the University intended to provide an

educated ministry for Calvinist congregations, and although the pious purpose does not completely account for its rapid rise, undoubtedly two major factors in its success were that it was fundamentally Protestant, and situated in a rich, busy commercial country. For those who would understand the University which meant so much in Elsevier history, it is profitable to follow the ramifications of the two influences upon it of business and Protestantism. Concerning the commercial factor, it almost goes without saying that institutions have more success if situated in rich cities than if founded elsewhere. Many colleges were founded under conditions as auspicious as the beginnings of Columbia University, but were unfortunate in choosing a location which did not develop into the great city of America. Scores of institutions in the midwest were founded before the University of Chicago, with purposes as high, by men equally unselfish; but they were not founded in strategic commercial locations and have remained small colleges. Leyden was analogous to our metropolitan universities, being founded in an industrial city in a country on the verge of great commercial expansion. Being financially able, Leyden could draw its faculty from other countries. Scaliger, Saumaise, and many others were induced to come to Leyden for what were considered high salaries. The use of Latin in the universities made this possible. In the year in which Elsevier came to Leyden three men on a faculty of nine came from outside the northern provinces. Ten years later (in 1590) there were professors who were natives to France, England, Scotland, Germany and Norway. The other factor, that of being a Protestant university in a Protestant-dominated land, also had its effect in attracting faculty. Joseph Juste Scaliger, the greatest scholar of his age, and Protestant, came to the University. The gray landscape chilled his spirit, he cursed the city as a swamp within a swamp, as has been said, but stayed and avowed he had never been treated more kindly. Another great scholar was Claude Saumaise (Salmasius). The bad climate wearied him, too, but he said he found at Leyden something he could not find in France, namely liberty and freedom of conscience. A third Frenchman, Pierre du Moulin, felt himself favorably disposed to accept a post at Leyden because it promised security, facilities for study, and an opportunity to serve his church.

Because the faculty was illustrious, students gathered from all over Europe. In the twenty-six years from 1575 to 1600, of the two thousand seven hundred and twenty-five students registered, forty-one per cent were from outside the United Provinces, from the southern Netherlands, Germany, France, England, Denmark, Poland, Scotland, Switzerland, Italy, Bohemia, Austria, Norway, and Sweden. In the twenty-five year period from 1601 to 1625, a little more than forty-three per cent of the six thousand three hundred and twenty-six students registered were foreigners, and in the twenty-five year period from 1626 to 1650 more than fifty-two per cent of the eleven thousand seventy-six students were from outside the United Provinces. By that time there were students from all of the countries which have been mentioned, and in addition students from Hungary, Spain, the Turkish Empire, the North African States, Ireland, and Persia.

But the operation of the two factors, Protestantism and capitalism, are most interestingly observed in the formation of the curricula. It is worthwhile in this connection to observe, however cursorily, the course of oriental and theological studies at Leyden. To this day the University is a renowned center for oriental studies. Its development was due to the interweaving of three factors, the two which have been mentioned, and the fact that the late sixteenth and the seventeenth century comprised the great era of scientific discovery. In that age there was a zest for mathematics, which had an extensive literature in Arabic. The three factors in the development of oriental studies are exemplified in the work of Scaliger, Golius, and the students of modern near-east languages. Scaliger was bent upon defending his faith against attacks of Catholic theologians. It occurred to him that all history had been written or annotated by Catholic writers in Catholic countries; the basic materials of controversy were in their hands. He set himself the task of re-examining the chronology of world history, searching Chaldaic, Arabic, and other Asiatic records for information on essential dates. He stressed to his students the necessity of going to the sources of ecclesiastical history, and one of the students, Thomas Erpenius, was among the foremost orientalists of his day. Golius exemplifies the impetus given to oriental studies by mathematics. As a student at Leyden, he intended to be a mathematician and astronomer, but in the attempt to get at scientific knowledge locked up in Arabic literature he drifted farther and farther away from mathematics, and eventually ended as an orientalist. The influence of the commercial community on oriental studies is apparent in several ways. Netherlanders, having their business on great waters, became practical philologists. The first vocabulary of the Malay language, for example, was published by Frederik de Houtman, a merchant and explorer, in 1603. In the seventeeth century Dutch merchants increasingly sent vessels into the Mediterranean and gathered trade into their hands. Commercial relations with Mediterranean peoples meant official relations with them. The States General maintained an official interpreter of oriental languages. Ravelinghen, Scaliger, Erpenius and Golius, all professors at Leyden, served in the office. It was said of both Golius and Erpenius that letters composed by them were admired by princes and dignitaries of the near east for the elegance of their Arabic style. In view of the extensive eastern trade, Erpenius proposed that a native of the near east be brought to Leyden to teach colloquial Arabic.

Turning from orientalists to theologians, it is apparent the vigorous Protestantism of Leyden professors had wide influence. The views of Arminius, one of the early rectors of the University, have transcended the boundaries of Holland and his own time. Sir Henry Wotton, who knew him at Leyden, judged him to be 'a man of most rare learning,' and 'knew him to be of a most strict life and of a most meek spirit.' This sincere man was unable to accept the doctrine of the more rigid Calvinists. It appeared to him, for example, that the idea of predestination implied that God had decided there was to be sin in the world, that therefore He had created sin, that He caused it to be committed, that He had thereby in a final analysis sinned Himself, which was a monstrous idea. The viewpoint of Arminius and his followers was that they could recognize no authority but the Bible; they denied that the problem of predestination had been clearly answered by that Authority, and that it was not fundamental to salvation. The party of Arminius was the party of the Remonstrants, and the quarrel of Remonstrant versus Contra-Remonstrant tore asunder the church in Holland. To some extent, although there were also political complications, it was the cause of the execution of one of Holland's greatest men, Oldenbarnevelt, and the exile of another, Hugo Grotius. The moving spirit of the Remonstrants was Arminius, a member of the University of Leyden, and the leading exponent of the opposition was Gomarus, likewise professor at Leyden.

Another influential University rector was Johannes Koch (Cocceius), who, following the spirit of his age, was inclined to take a reasonable, tolerant view of theology. Both Latitudinarians of the Anglican church and Pietists among German Lutherans have found some of their origins in Dutch Protestantism. In both movements, so different in nature, Koch, in his time, played a part. One aim of Pietism was to free religion from the tyranny of formalism and dogma, and this, too, was an aim of Latitudinarianism. But whereas both movements minimized formalism, thereafter their routes parted: Latitudinarianism valued a minimum of formalism because it permitted a wide, reasonable view of religion, acceptable to all; Pietism valued a minimum of dogma and government since it permitted intense individual religious experience. In the tendency toward simplification and tolerance Koch was a leader. Like Arminius, he looked to the Bible rather than to the church for guidance, and was able to prove to his own satisfaction there was no need for a Christian to observe the Sabbath. Koch had for a student Lodenstein, called the first of the Pietists; and Theodore Untereyk at Mulhaus, another early German Pietist, spoke of himself as ploughing with the oxen of Koch. Anglicans have asserted the beginnings of Latitudinarianism are to be found in Dutch theology. German Lutherans are satisfied that Pietism sprang from the same source. The reaction to the first was in part Methodist evangelism; the reaction to the second was rationalism; so, speaking broadly, the influence of Leyden theologians, living and working during the time of the Elseviers, lasted, however attenuated, well into the eighteenth century.

It is not possible, of course, to describe in a few paragraphs a great university's activities over a century, but even a few paragraphs are better than none. The Elseviers published classical authors which students needed; they provided themselves with oriental types to publish researches of orientalists; they printed polemics of Remonstrants and Counter-Remonstrants, of Stevin of the Engineering School, of the distinguished exiles, Scaliger and Saumaise. Perhaps, at least, a glimpse has been given of the vigorous intellectual life of Leyden and what it could mean to a bookseller and publisher.

2

Louis Elsevier at Leyden

THE city census of 1581 duly took note of the fact that one Louis Elsevier, a binder of Louvain, now resided in Leyden, and that he had brought with him an assistant, Pauls Reyniers, also of Louvain. The new man was soon at work binding books for the University (there are books bound by him still in the University library), and as opportunities developed he made an honest guilder in other phases of the book business. But the caliber of the men engaged in book trades was high, and competition keen. There were in Leyden, for example, during the years Louis worked there, dealers who also were recognized writers, and the prestige of authorship made them respected rivals. Jan Janszoon Orlers, who wrote a history of Leyden among other works, was printer, publisher and dealer in the town from 1596 to 1616, and his shop was a gathering place for scholars and travelers. Hendrik van Haestens, another Elsevier competitor in the years 1598 to 1629, was the author of two books and collaborated with Orlers on a third. His description of *The Grim and Bloody Siege of the City of Ostend in Flanders* was subsequently published by Elsevier. In addition to authors, there were other formidable competitors. Jan Jacobszoon Paedts, both printer and bookseller, stood high in the community. He had been banished for his Calvinist faith while Leyden was still under Catholic domination but returned in 1569 to devote most of his efforts to printing religious works and Bibles. Another contemporary, Jan Bouwenszoon, had been established at Leyden since 1571. He strove for the type of business that interested Elsevier, printing books by and for university men. He continued to work until 1608. There were also men who excelled as craftsmen, like Cornelis Hackius, who began work in 1608, and together with other members of the family made the Hackius establishment one of the best in Europe.

Since Elsevier aimed at university trade, possibly the keenest competition was offered by the printers to the University. The first of these was Willem Silvius. In 1569 this stout Calvinist, while still working at Antwerp, had the acumen or good luck to publish the epigrams of a young scholar, Johan van der Does, who a few years later became a hero of the siege of Leyden, and what is more to the point, a curator of the new University. It is not difficult to conjecture how it came about that in June, 1577, 'for the improvement of the University and the convenience and accommodation of the students' Silvius was named typographer, bookseller, and printer general to the University. He entered upon his duties in 1579, before Elsevier arrived in Leyden. In addition to his duties as printer he was to provide such books published by others as the University needed. After Silvius' death in 1580 the office was passed first to his son Karel and then to the great Christopher Plantin, who had dealings with the University from about the year of Silvius' death. In April, 1581, through Professor Lipsius, Plantin asked the Senate for a copy of the University seal so that he might have a stamp made to mark the books he gave to the institution. His prestige, his powerful friend on the faculty, Justus

Lipsius, and his conscious cultivation of the University worked in his favor. He was named official printer in May, 1584, the commission to be effective from May, 1583. When Parma had again made Antwerp a comfortable place for Catholics, Plantin, who seemed able to remain on good terms with Spanish and natives, Protestants and Catholics, returned there in August, 1585. He left his printing plant at Leyden to his son-in-law, François Ravelinghen, who was named printer in his place in March, 1586, and extraordinary professor of Hebrew in June of the same year. After Ravelinghen's death his son, Christoffel, held the post from 1597 to 1600, and in 1602 the old Leyden resident, Paedts, was appointed.

Altogether, within the period 1550–99, forty-four printers and booksellers are known to have been established in Leyden, and in the period 1600 to 1624 there were sixty-one. It was into this world of printers who were professors, authors who sold books, bookmen who were officials of the University, that Elsevier projected himself. He was experienced and resourceful. During his lifetime at Leyden he explored all branches of the book business that promised profit: bookbinding, bookselling, book auctions, publishing, traveling book salesman; and he added to these multifarious activities the duties of University beadle. The variety of his efforts is indicative of the hard fight to establish himself. There are other signs that his road was a rough one. He was able to procure a house adjacent to the University where he could retail books to students and professors, but the book stock for the establishment he procured from Christopher Plantin only by incurring an obligation of one thousand two hundred and seventy guilders. He acknowledged the debt before the magistrates in September, 1583, agreeing to an initial payment of seventy guilders, the remainder to be paid at the rate of twenty-five guilders per month. If the payments were not made, Plantin was to take his house on the Rapenburg, then his house in the Kloksteeg, and, in general, all of his goods. This Plantin-Elsevier agreement indicates Elsevier was in the book business in 1583. Additional proof is offered by a treatise published in that year, written by Drusius, Leyden professor of Hebrew, Chaldaic and Syriac, which carries on the errata leaf the information that the book could be purchased at the place of Louis Elsevier near the University.

Booksellers find to their sorrow that a university clientele is hard to please, at times their only requirement regarding books seeming to be that they be published in a foreign country and hard to get. The Leyden University population had the penchant well developed. When Jan Paedts was appointed University printer, for example, it was specified that in addition to his duties as printer he should bring back from the Frankfurt book fair, 'at his own cost and peril,' such books as curators, professors, and other notable members of the University desired, and that he should sell them to the illuminati at a rate of exchange agreed upon beforehand. The Amsterdam booksellers were trading at Frankfurt even before Paedts at Leyden was required to do so, and to meet the competition of his Leyden and Amsterdam contemporaries Elsevier was soon a regular visitor at the fair also.

Dealers from all over Europe congregated at Frankfurt twice a year to buy and sell, and the stocks on display attracted scholars as well as booksellers. 'Who,' asked Henri Estienne, writing of the fair in 1574, 'when he sees himself surrounded by so many learned writers, would not suppose that he was in Athens? In the shops of the book-

sellers one hears men discussing philosophy no less seriously than once Socrates and Plato discussed it in the
Lyceum. And there are not only philosophers there; the
celebrated universities of Vienna, Wittenberg, Leipzig,
Heidelberg and Strassburg, the foreign universities of
Louvain, Padua, Oxford, Cambridge, and many others
too numerous to mention, send to the Fair not only their
philosophers but also their poets, orators, historians,
mathematicians, and some who are skilled in all branches
of learning.' The fair was highly organized, and a class of
merchants developed who made a business of selling at
Frankfurt the books printed by associates in their home
cities or countries. Elsevier became such a broker. He not
only took his own publications and book stock to the fair,
but also acted for Haestens, Orlers, Cloucq, and Van der
Bild of Leyden; Abraham van der Rade of Leeuwarden;
Salomon le Roy of Utrecht; Richard Schilders of Middelburg; and Laurentius of Amsterdam. He was first represented in the fair catalogues in 1595, his name occurring
again in 1597 and 1599. In a letter to Adrien van der Meer,
dated 29 November 1601, Janus Gruterus, renowned
professor of Heidelberg, advised his correspondent about
mail service. 'Your letters,' he said, 'will be delivered to
me if you hand them over to Mr Elsevier, the bookseller,
who comes to the Frankfurt Fair every year.'

In February, 1602, Elsevier asked and obtained permission from the rector and academic senate to be absent
from his duties as beadle to travel for three months in
Germany and France, and Gruterus mentioned in a letter
to Meursius in June of the same year that he had again
seen Elsevier at Frankfurt. The fair catalogue for the
following year showed that Elsevier occupied a stall in
conjunction with George Willer, bookseller of Augsburg.

23

After that date his name appeared in fair catalogues as an independent trader. Apparently he continued to make the journey to Frankfurt for many years, since in April, 1612, Gruterus again wrote to Meursius to say that, 'Elsevier, that fine fellow, has gotten Leo's *Tactica* for me all right.'

Louis was also known at Louvain, for Puteanus, a famous professor there, in writing to Daniel Heinsius in November, 1609, asked to be remembered to Elsevier. He was also assiduous in cultivating trade in Paris. Pierre L'Estoile, a French bibliophile, entered in his journal for August, 1609, that, 'On Thursday, the twenty-seventh, a Dutch bookdealer from Leyden named Elsevier whom I have known for a long time brought me the following three bagatelles which have been recently issued at Leyden. *The Freedom of the Seas*, by Hugo Grotius, *Congratulatory Poems of Dominicus Baudius dedicated in honour of the Duke of Spinola* (which is pure twaddle), and the *Memorial* to the great Scaliger ... which contains the learned and elegant funeral orations of Heinsius and Baudius, in the second of which, by Baudius, I remarked two or three notable things which Baudius cited as evidence of Scaliger's pious and religious life ... Before that oration there is a copy of the bequest which he made to the University of Leyden library of his Greek, Hebrew, Chaldaic, Syriac, Arabic, Ethiopian, Persian, and Armenian manuscripts. Elsevier tells me that the Leyden gentlemen esteem that present to be worth three thousand crowns. Although he did not wish to take it, I gave Elsevier half a crown for the books.' In addition to selling books in Paris, Elsevier bought volumes there to take to Holland. In Scaliger's opinion he brought back the wrong ones. 'You should know,' the latter wrote to a friend in 1608, 'that the books which are printed in your city arrive here in Leyden very late or never. Since he does most of his business at The Hague, Elsevier loads himself up at Paris with legal forms and law books.' The remark is interesting as an indication that Elsevier went frequently to Paris, but should not be taken too seriously. Scaliger's complaint is remarkably like that of his distinguished contemporary, Casaubon. 'If I ask you,' wrote Casaubon in 1595 to his friend Commelin at Heidelberg, 'to send me direct all that issues from your press, it is not, believe me, dearest Commelin, because I am unwilling to buy them, but because I am unable. Our booksellers here (at Geneva) are a blind lot who don't care to bring back from Frankfurt what they think will not pay.'

Elsevier's career as publisher developed later than his bookselling activities. Before 1594 only one book appeared with his imprint; but afterward, with the exception of 1600, he published at least one book a year, in later years sometimes ten books appearing with the Elsevier imprint. Like contemporary publishers, those of seventeenth-century Holland often specialized. There were those who sold chapbooks and newsbooks; those who catered to the trade of French exiles, who sought the business of learned professions, or who aimed to supply the shipping world with charts and books on navigation. Elsevier was of the group of dealers and publishers specializing in books for the learned. By far the greater number, more than ninety-six per cent, of his books were in Latin; and the most consistent producers of books published by him were professors, notably Meursius, Baudius, and Puteanus. Occasionally he issued books in conjunction with other dealers, sometimes both names appearing on the title-page, at other times the name of one being on part of the edition, and the name of the other on the remainder. In some instances also, Elsevier merely acted as agent for publications of others. In all, about one hundred and three publications were issued by Louis Elsevier, or partly at his expense, or labeled as being sold at his shop. Without stretching imagination too far, a number of these might be termed best sellers. A poem, *Alexandra*, usually ascribed to the minor Greek poet Lycophron, and beloved by pedants, went through two editions, and Meursius' Greek glossary likewise had two editions. A most successful work was one which had been popular before being added to Elsevier's list. This was by John Dickenson and entitled *The Tragic Mirror, comprising in brief the ruins and the calamitous endings of the foremost kings, dukes and lords of the past century, in which divine judgments and also human frailty are explained by outstanding examples*. Two of the books mentioned were of interest to students and professors, and the volume of calamitous and sensational tidings would have had wide appeal. Present-day publishers would agree that school books and sensational news are likely to be successful ventures.

Elsevier had his share of duds also. An oration by Antoine Arnauld attacking Jesuits was published in 1594 but did not go well. The year following it was given a new title, some minor additions were made, and thus refurbished it was given another try. A work by a Leyden geographer, Filip Cluver, on the mouths of the Rhine, and Pieter Schrijver's collection of writings on the Netherlands, both of which had evidently not sold well as separate publications, were smartened up with a new title-page and issued as a single new work. Elsevier employed this technique on more than one occasion, and he used new title-pages, also, to brighten up single works when sales were sluggish. Such operations would doubtless be frowned upon by the Harvard School of Business, but life was real and earnest in seventeenth-century Holland. In general the tone of commerce was set by the desperately hard world of international trade, where every man's hand was against his neighbor, and where an ethical business man might find ruin as the only reward for virtue. Much later Sir William Temple observed that Holland was a place where 'a man would choose rather to travel than to live, where ... profit is more in request than honour.' In an age when they were general, Elsevier's sharp practices cannot be judged too harshly.

Probably his familiarity with the book world helped Elsevier to be appointed University beadle. In January, 1586, he was instrumental in procuring for the University library a valuable manuscript collection of classic inscriptions which, during its colorful history, had been stolen by a band of Englishmen. The grateful University awarded Elsevier one hundred guilders, partly to reimburse him for the expense he had been at, and partly to show appreciation for the manner in which he handled the affair. Soon after, the University was faced with the selection of a beadle, a man who could get about and transact the necessary institutional business. What could be more natural than to select the skilled negotiator, the local bookseller? On 8 December, 1586, he officially assumed the office. On that day he proceeded to the Town Hall of Leyden and took the oath of office at the hands of Johan van der Does, Curator of the University. He promised to render due honor and reverence to the honorable rector and the academic senate, to obey all instructions given him by these dignitaries, to do his utmost to preserve the good name of the University, and

27

in short to do all that a good, sincere, and faithful beadle ought to do. It should be explained that the beadle was usher, doorkeeper, messenger, and something of a secretary. If the rector wished to send letters to The Hague, Elsevier was entrusted with them. When the academic senate was disturbed about the hour Baudius, the colorful professor of eloquence, proposed to conduct classes, they sent Elsevier looking for the erring instructor. When, in 1591, the curators wished to invite Franciscus Junius to the chair of theology, they sent the beadle to Heidelberg with the invitation. On solemn academic occasions, he marched in procession carrying his mace of office, as befitted an important, dignified official. The rector entered among his expenses for 22 January, 1591, the sum of nine guilders for wine poured at the wedding of Louis' second son, 'An occasion,' the rector wrote in his expense account, 'on which many professors were present,' indicating that Elsevier had at last scaled the dizzy heights of academic society.

But friendship with the scholarly great and the multiplication of activities did not mean that Elsevier had been living a success story. He had been unable, as a matter of fact, to repay his old debt to Plantin, with the result that in April, 1586, he was forced to sell both his house on the Rapenburg and his home on the Kloksteeg to the famous man, although he continued to occupy his house until May of the following year. The loss of the property was a serious blow, since it was from the house on the Rapenburg that he conducted a retail book trade with the students. Elsevier immediately endeavored to re-establish himself; in April, 1587, the humble and obedient servitor of the University, their beadle and bookseller, presented a petition to the curators. He related that for six years he had done all he could to live near the University so that he might bind and sell books for the benefit of students. In the very next month, the petitioner continued, he would be forced to give up his shop on the Rapenburg near the University. He would then be compelled to betake himself, to the great detriment of business, to a strange, distant quarter where he would be unable to conduct trade under favorable circumstances, a matter of great importance to him. It was for these reasons the petitioner addressed himself to the University curators 'to the end that if it please you, you may grant him as a special favor a small place in the University near the street where he might construct a small shop, as you granted four years ago to Christopher Plantyn, this plot to be of such a size as you shall deem fit.' The curators considered the matter and eventually granted the right to build a shop immediately inside the University gate, with the proviso that Elsevier tear it down when asked to do so.

The unfortunate result of the debt to Plantin occurred in 1586. As late as 1594 Elsevier still had a struggle to remain in business. On 15 August of that year two notes he had signed came due, one being guaranteed by John Moretus, son-in-law of Plantin, for seventy-six guilders ten *stuivers*, and the other for sixty guilders, guaranteed by Gilles Beys, another Plantin son-in-law. On the date the notes matured the holder of the paper, Thomas de Vechter, a typefounder, went to Elsevier's house on the Rapenburg accompanied by a notary and two witnesses. The notary reported that after desultory talk which was not much to the point, Elsevier exclaimed, 'Even if I had the money there before me on the table I would not pay it. I have acknowledged the debt, and I do so now, but wait eight or ten days until my son Gillis, whom I expect at any moment, returns from Frisia.' But De Vechter was impatient for his money and demanded the guarantors make payment of interest, damages and principal. Now the sums in question, sixty and seventy-six guilders, were not large (a first-class scholar like Scaliger was paid two thousand guilders a year) and yet evidently they were inconveniently large sums for Elsevier at the time. Soon after, his affairs took a turn for the better. On 8 August, 1594, he was admitted *burger*, or citizen of Leyden, being guaranteed by his son Mathijs, who had become a citizen a few days previously. From that time his business prospered. He published increasing numbers of books, and there are extant no further indications he was short of money.

About 1601 Elsevier developed an original method of turning a profit. It had been customary for dealers at book fairs to auction their remainders when the fairs ended to save the trouble of transporting them home again. In the year mentioned, Elsevier gave a new turn to the device by auctioning the library of a rich merchant, Daniel van der Meulen, where about twelve hundred items brought two thousand eight hundred guilders. Later (1604) the collections of George and Johan van der Does were auctioned, and after the death of Scaliger, in 1604, his books also went under the hammer. These sales were followed by that of the library of Vulcanius, a fine classical scholar, and one of the first of Germanic philologists. One part of this library was offered in November, 1610, and another in June, 1615, after the death of the owner. Book auctions continued to be held by Louis' descendants both at Leyden and at the branch at The Hague.

It is interesting to speculate upon the personality of this bookseller, publisher, auctioneer, and beadle. It would not be difficult to show that the number of printers in the southern provinces who stood manfully by their Calvinist beliefs and were sent into exile, to the galleys, or to jail for their pains, was large. Van Waesberghe migrated to Rotterdam, Silvius and Ravelinghen to Leyden. Many were banished from Antwerp or stood in the stocks in the city. But there were others who quickly conformed to whatever ideas were dominant at the moment. It can at least be claimed for Elsevier that he belonged to the segment of the population showing character and courage. It is obvious also that he was a competent man of business; a concern which could suffer as many displacements as did Elsevier's and yet be found ultimately among the leaders in the field is one which has had competent management. Elsevier was sharp in business practice, but not unusually so for his time. To the impression of a successful merchant, we can add that of a man with a sense of humor. The old Netherlands cities were divided into neighborhoods, for each of which a chief or factotum was elected at a mass meeting of neighbors. Leyden was divided into seventy-seven such quarters, and Elsevier was chief of his neighborhood which was whimsically known as the Kingdom of Gravensteyn. It was his duty to settle disputes, to maintain the peace, and to take charge of the night guard. As neighborhood leader, he also collected various small dues, assessments on families moving into the neighborhood, and on couples being married, for example. The tolls so collected were expended on an annual general feast. On the occasion of the feast, Elsevier issued a burlesque proclamation which began, 'Louis Elsevier, by the Grace of God, Lord of the New Kingdom of Gravensteyn, Ruler and Lord-proprietor of the East side of the Rapenburg canal, of the south side of Wood Street, and of the West side of Saint Peter's Churchyard together with Clock Alley, Margrave of the meadow canal, and baron of the state timber wharf . . .' Following the impressive introduction Elsevier outlined the rules governing the festivities.

As the end of his life approached, Louis had cause for satisfaction. He was the father of six sons, five of whom were living, and of two daughters. He possessed a good business, wide acquaintance abroad, and a firm university connection. His sons increasingly took part in the business. In 1608, for example, a contribution to the interminable debates between Jesuits and Calvinists was published by his sixth son, Bonaventura; and in 1610 the same son issued the Poetics of Aristotle. Since 1607 the oldest son, Mathijs, had been also beadle of the University; the second son, Louis, managed the branch store at The Hague from 1590; and Gillis, the third son, also had been employed for a time at The Hague establishment. Joost, the fourth son, was a bookseller at Utrecht in the period from 1603 to 1616. But during his lifetime Louis and his sons were barred from the desirable post of University printer since they were booksellers only and not printers. It was not until 1616, the year before Louis Elsevier's death, that a member of his family, his grandson Isaac, owned printing equipment, and it was three years after his death that the grandson became University printer, the first Elsevier to hold the office.

The last days of the sturdy old fighter were saddened by a calamitous fire which broke out on 11 November, 1616, and destroyed the greater part of the University building in which public lectures were held. An investigation fixed responsibility on the beadles, Louis and his son Mathijs. The case of Louis was held in abeyance, but Mathijs' was decided almost immediately. When the academic senate met on Tuesday, November 22, it was first resolved to resume classes on the following Monday, and then the senate rendered the opinion that 'Mathijs should be suspended from his office until he should either prove his innocence or should admit his guilt with regard to the fire which destroyed the Academy and thereupon receive forgiveness.' Accordingly he was suspended. The family calamity was a heavy blow for an old man who had taken many. He died soon after, being in his seventieth or seventy-first year. He was buried on 4 February, 1617, in Saint Peter's Church beside his wife, Mayke Duverdyn, his companion on exiles and travels, who had died three years previously.

3

The Elseviers at The Hague, Utrecht and Leyden

THE Elseviers were a large clan. Louis had nine children, and among these, their children, their grandchildren, and their great-grandchildren, there were fourteen who were booksellers, or printers, or both. The records of the multitude, their births, deaths, loves (insofar as they resulted in marriage), business transactions, and minor villainies are scattered through official records in the cities where they lived. The Elsevier businesses at The Hague and Utrecht were founded during the lifetime of Louis. It is of interest to follow the story of those who worked in these cities, as well as those who succeeded Louis at Leyden.

The chronology of The Hague shop can be briefly given. Founded probably in 1590 by Louis, the second son, it endured until about 1665 or later. At least eight Elseviers were concerned in its operation. The younger Louis ran it (except for a brief period when his brother Gillis took his place) from the date of its founding until his death in 1620. It was inherited by his younger brother, Bonaventura, who almost immediately after coming into possession assigned it to his nephew for a consideration of two hundred and forty guilders. The nephew, Jacob Elsevier, fell heir to a fortune of four thousand pounds which allowed him to take a less enthusiastic view of trade than the Elseviers were usually able to take. Nine years after the windfall he quit active business, and control of the shop passed to his brother Abraham, who, from the year 1637 or 1638, directed its affairs in addition to his main concern, the printing and bookselling establishment at Leyden. At Abraham's death in 1652 the businesses in Leyden and The Hague were inherited by his son Johannes. There is evidence of an irresolute, erratic streak in the Elseviers, and Johannes had it. In 1659-60 he sold his book stock at Leyden, and after his death his wife conducted a sale of books from the shop at The Hague (1661). The rent for the shop in the Great Hall for the period from 1662 to 1666 was paid by Louis and Daniël Elsevier of Amsterdam, and in the latter year, or in 1665, it passed into the hands of Daniël Steucker. These are the essentials of the story of The Hague shop, but several details in the establishment's history are worth mentioning. First of all, there was logic in founding a branch in the city. Traditionally the great users of books are preachers, lawyers, and professors. At Leyden the Elseviers were already exploiting the theological and professorial market, and inevitably discovered the lawyers and government officials at The Hague. The town, 'the pleasantest village that is in Europe,' said George Gascoigne, rapidly gained prestige as the seat of government. Foreign travelers were charmed by it. John Evelyn, who was there in 1641, ' . . . went to visit the Hoff, or Prince's court, with the adjoining gardens full of ornament, close walks, statues, marbles, grots, fountains, and artificial music.' Samuel Pepys, visiting there twenty years later, 15 May, 1660, declared ' . . . I cannot speak enough of the gallantry of the town,' and added, 'Everybody of fashion speaks French or Latin, or both. The women many of them very pretty and in good habits, fashionable and black spots.' 'It was,' he concluded, 'a most sweet town with bridges and a river in every street.' In 1594, not many years after arriving in The Hague, young Louis Elsevier bought a house on the Spuibrug and rented two stalls in the *Groote Zaal*, or Great Hall, in the Binnenhof, which at the time was beginning to fill with shops. In the seventeenth century it was common to find shops in churches, palaces, and public buildings. There were shops in Westminster Hall, for example, and Saint Paul's Churchyard was once the center of the London book trade. In Denmark, until well into the eighteenth century, a church was a fitting and proper place for a book stall; and Henry IV of France, in his conscious effort to stimulate manufacture, lodged in his palace of the Louvre, printers, sculptors, watchmakers, perfumers, cutlers, armorers, gilders, damasceners, tapestry workers, and instrument makers. The renting, then, of shops and stalls in the courtyard and great hall of the Counts of Holland was not unusual. By 1614, and perhaps from its inception, the Elseviers had the largest establishment in the Hall, two stalls with a total length of forty-two feet for which they paid the highest rent, twelve pounds per annum.

A stall in the Hall was well placed to catch the trade of the learned and polite world. Those high and mighty gentlemen, the members of the States General, and the great mighty members of the States of Holland and West Frisia could be counted upon to visit the Hall. Courtiers, lawyers, and officials found it conveniently at hand; and foreign gentlemen, on diplomatic business, or merely in Holland as tourists, sooner or later visited it. Evelyn was there and reported that 'There is to this palace a stately hall, not much inferior to ours of Westminster, hung round with colours and other trophies taken from the Spaniards;

and the sides below are furnished with shops.' Pepys went also to gaze and admire, and found the Hall ' . . . a great place, where the flags that they take from their enemies are all hung up; and things to be sold, as in Westminster Hall, and not much unlike it, but that not so big, but much neater.' Perhaps the two English gentlemen stopped at the Elsevier shop, for Pepys had infinite curiosity about a number of things, and Evelyn highly regarded the fame of the Elseviers.

The stalls were not an immediate success, and young Louis Elsevier experienced difficult times. This is suggested in a letter to Meursius (dated shortly before Louis died) in which Meursius' correspondent wrote, 'In the matter of the books from the library of the late Mr Huisman which were sold at public auction, Louis Elsevier still has not discharged his debt. I ask you to urge him to do this so that the tutors will not be forced to resort to extreme measures.' A petition addressed by Elsevier's widow to the Court of Justice in the year of his death also suggests he had not been affluent. In forwarding the petition to his superiors, Luchtenburch, the functionary in charge of renting stalls, explained that Louis had agreed to pay twelve pounds one *stuiver* rent per year for two stalls and to pay two pounds for each book auction held. But although asked to pay many times in the two years preceding his death, that is in 1618 and 1619, he had paid neither rent nor auction fees for those years. When his widow was asked about payment, she declared she had no means, 'which,' says Luchtenburch, 'I understand to be true, for he was very fond of drinking wine.' This officer recommended that since the widow was burdened with debts and was getting no profit, out of respect for her widowhood, she should be forgiven the money she owed the court.

But if the bookstalls were not brilliantly successful it was not because Louis and others of the family lacked imagination and enterprise. In 1596 Louis obtained the right to hold book auctions in the Great Hall, and for many years, in fact until 1643, this privilege remained a family monopoly. He also obtained, in 1619, the privilege to publish the official French editions of the judgments rendered against Johan van Oldenbarnevelt, Rombout Hogerbeets, Gilles van Ledenbergh, and Hugo Grotius. Throughout the life of the concern books were sold to the provincial court of justice, the earliest recorded sale being in 1596 when it was ordered that Louis Elsevier be paid three hundred and sixty pounds for books furnished that body. Jacob Elsevier continued the connection with the court, and in addition sold books to the municipal government, being so influential with the city fathers it was forbidden to use or to buy Latin or Greek schoolbooks in The Hague which did not contain his mark.

That the municipality relied on them for such schoolbooks indicates the Elseviers enjoyed a pre-eminent place in the learned book trade. Occasionally they went to great lengths to protect the position. Once they tried to prevent Jan Barentszoon, who also sold learned books, from taking a stall in the Hall. The effort in restraint of trade came to the attention of the officials, and Luchtenburch (the same officer who handled the petition of Louis' wife) rendered a report on the matter. According to Luchtenburch, one, Jacques Fernandes, had rented two stalls in the Great Hall and, following his death, his wife wished to rent one of them to Jan Barentszoon, son of a bookseller at Amsterdam. Elsevier (whether Jacob or Bonaventura is not clear) succeeded in getting all shopkeepers in the Hall to protest the entrance of Barentszoon. They declared to Luchtenburch they would all be ruined if he were allowed to rent space. But Luchtenburch avowed he could not imagine how 'spectacle makers, button makers, ribbon sellers, hosiery makers, brush makers, and others should be ruined who had nothing in common with the selling of books.' And even the booksellers, he added, with the exception of Elsevier, would not be affected since 'they would not sell in a whole year three books like those which will be sold by Barentszoon.' In Luchtenburch's opinion the disturbance was due to the fact that since his father was a large scale printer at Amsterdam, Barentszoon was able to sell books cheaper than Elsevier, a fact that Elsevier admitted. Luchtenburch supported his view by saying certain officials complained to him that since Elsevier had no competitors he sold books so dear it was difficult to do business with him. He added that an Amsterdam lawyer bought books from Barentszoon for seventy-two pounds that Elsevier declared he would not sell for less than one hundred and ten, and a book for which Elsevier asked sixty pounds could be gotten from Barentszoon for thirty-two. Luchtenburch recommended to the court, both because he believed those who used scholarly books should be favored and because he regarded it as bad policy to yield to pressure of shop renters, that Jan Barentszoon be allowed to have a place in the Hall, and this was accordingly done.

The Great Hall was a desirable location since booksellers there enjoyed advantages over their competitors in the town. In European cities of the period judicial and administrative systems sometimes contained anomalies due to ancient legal and administrative jurisdictions enjoyed by the church and hereditary lords. This was the case at The Hague, for although the courtyard and the

Great Hall were within the city, the grounds and buildings were the ancient properties of the Counts of Holland. At the time of revolution the rights of the last count, Philip II, devolved upon the States of Holland. As a consequence, booksellers in the Hall maintained, and successfully, that they were not subject to the restrictions of the city gild of booksellers and printers, but only to the will of officers whom the States set over them. The strife between booksellers of city and Hall endured for decades. Some Hague dealers found it wise to protect themselves against what they considered unfair trade practices of Hall retailers by taking stalls there themselves; but a number of merchants in the Hall, the Elseviers among them, never became gild members. An especially sore point with city booksellers was the holding of book auctions in the Hall, a practice they considered cut-throat and outrageous. Until 1643 the Elseviers were the only booksellers holding auctions; inevitably they harassed regular Hague bookmen. How tradesmen felt about auctions is made clear in a complaint which, in 1646, they begged leave to lay before the high and mighty gentlemen of the Chamber of the Treasurer's accounts for the Count of Holland. The booksellers drew attention to the fact that the number of book auctions was increasing daily, and especially those held in the Great Hall. The books for these sales were brought from various foreign and distant towns and countries, and what is more, they were brought in and sold by one person alone (by whom they may have meant Elsevier). 'And the result is,' the plaintiffs continued, 'that those who have been everywhere endeavoring to sell books, when they find that other cities will not allow them to do business because of the harm which it might do to the citizens, they bring their books to The Hague and sell as they please, no sooner finishing one lot than beginning on the next one. All of this tends to bring about the total ruin, decay and injury of the petitioners, who thus impelled to do so can only submissively remonstrate . . . ' The plaintiffs recommended that auctions of books brought into the town be prohibited; that auctions be permitted only of such books as became available in The Hague by the death of inhabitants, as was the custom in other towns; and that booksellers, printers, and those who held auctions be allowed to issue catalogues only on condition they swear the books advertised were also readily available at The Hague. These measures, the suppliants continued, were necessary in order that they might be treated as were inhabitants of other cities, that they might live and flourish, not only for the welfare of themselves and their children, but in service, honor and respect for the great mighty gentlemen of the Chamber. The latter gentlemen harkened to the booksellers' pleadings to the extent of deciding no one should hold an auction in the Great Hall without asking and being granted permission to do so. Both Abraham Elsevier and Verhoeven, another merchant who had recently been granted the privilege of auctioneering, were notified of the new rule and also informed that they were required to submit a list of books to be auctioned and to give assurance that such books could be procured in town.

The position of Hague booksellers was especially difficult since the Great Hall presented an administrative anomaly, but in general their misfortunes were common to all Dutch bookmen. The Groningen dealers in 1619 complained of interlopers who sold bound and unbound books of all kinds and held public auctions. They did so again in 1626, and there were similar protests in Leyden and Franeker. In 1599 members of the bookmen's gild at Middelburg (in Zeeland) bewailed the fact 'that daily foreign itinerants and peddlers sell, along the street and at the Bourse, almanacs, little songs, and little books which they bring from [the Province of] Holland.' Similarly there were complaints, by those interested, against auctions of paintings and art objects. The fact of the matter was that wielders of political power were not interested in protecting printers, artists, or anyone who created or manufactured goods. The country was in the hands of traders, not manufacturers, who intended not to protect home industry, but to insure a supply of cheap goods which could successfully meet competition in foreign markets. The outcry of skilled craftsmen, of small manufacturers, against unfair competition was quite generally disregarded. When the Hague printers and booksellers complained about price cutting, auctions, and the importation of foreign books, they merely added their voices to those of an ineffectual multitude.

There were very few Elsevier publications issued at The Hague. In 1594 a piece appeared with the awkward title, *The answer of the Lords of the States General of the Netherlands Provinces to the letter of the Archduke of Austria which is appended, together with the proposals made by the Archduke to the States General*, which carried with it information that it could be bought from Louis Elsevier, bookseller in The Hague. A Latin edition of Linschoten's voyages, printed at The Hague (1599), in part at the cost of the author, also carried information in the imprint the book was being sold by Gillis Elsevier. The judgments against Oldenbarnevelt, Hogerbeets, Ledenbergh, and Grotius, before referred to, also carried warnings to the public that the only authentic copies were those to be had from Elsevier.

In 1610 Louis published *The Repentance of John Haren and his return to the Church of God*. The items mentioned, together with three editions of sine, tangent, and secant tables, practically completed the Hague list. The items were spread over the period from 1594 to 1629. After 1637, when the bookstalls came under direct control of the Leyden firm, which possessed printing equipment, there was no logical reason for publishing at the branch establishment.

In comparison with the Hague bookstalls, Elsevier activities at Utrecht were much less important and details concerning them more meager. Joost, fourth son of the original Louis, established himself there, officially becoming a citizen in September, 1600, and doing a book business at the sign of the Red Goose. Little else is known about him except that he sold books to the city library, the municipal accounts containing the following entries:

For the years 1603–4: 'To Joost Elzevier, bookseller, citizen of this city, in payment for various books and works which he has furnished to the inspectors for the library of the city, 128 pounds 13 shillings.'

For the years 1604–5: 'To Joost Elzevier, bookseller, for the works of Seneca, purchased from him by the commissioners and school inspectors of this city for their use 10 pounds 10 shillings.'

For the years 1605–6: 'To Joost Elzevier for the works of Bellarmine, purchased from him and deposited in the Saint Jans Library 26 pounds.'

In 1604 Joost was elected one of the 'deacons' of the printers, binders, and booksellers gild, and was still doing business as a bookseller in April, 1616, six months before his death.

43

Many years later Pieter Elsevier, grandson of Joost, was also bookseller and publisher at Utrecht. The minutes of the Broad Council for 3 June, 1667, contain information that 'The petition of Pieter Elsevier requested that he be allowed to conduct here his business consisting principally of unbound books. The gentlemen delegated to investigate the matter have examined the protest of the gild, and have reported to the Broad Council. The Broad Council following the presentation of this report have consented to allow Elsevier to handle or sell only unbound books and he is not empowered to sell any bound book, nor to bind up his unbound stock, nor to have them bound in his house, either directly or indirectly, under pain of a fine of one hundred guilders, which the suppliant shall be forced to pay for each offense. This fine shall be divided equally between the officer, the gild, and the informer. It is understood also that there will be no auction sales of unbound books, except after Elsevier's death; and with this understanding, those of the gild are ordered to receive Elsevier into their organization as a bookseller upon payment of the customary fees.' Apparently the action of the council was unsatisfactory to Elsevier, or the gild, or both, for the next month (on 22 July) the council modified its previous order, giving additional advantages to both Elsevier and the gild. The Broad Council decreed that Elsevier 'shall be authorized to buy and sell unbound books only; that he shall be invited to the public sales which take place before the board; and that he shall be required to clear his house of his binding equipment and of the bound books which he does not need within fourteen days from the promulgation of the ruling upon pain of suffering the penalty heretofore provided.'

It was unfortunate Pieter elected to sell books at Utrecht

in these particular years. In a sense, he ran athwart the desires of Louis XIV of France, who, planning to conquer the Netherlands, made the capture of Utrecht a subsidiary objective. In 1672, Louis' great armies under the brilliant generals Condé and Vauban, embarked on a war which, in the beginning, was a triumphant march. Utrecht surrendered to the French in June, 1672, without a blow, and the French Intendant, Robert, placed in charge of the city, began systematically to milk the town of all wealth it possessed, stripping the homes of rich burghers of their last rickety chairs and worn tapestries. 'I am sure,' this *gauleiter* wrote to Louvois, Louis' minister of war, 'that if you were present you would never permit all the cruelties I commit upon these people to get from them the little money I do.' Louvois replied that he had 'received the account of the contributions. The total sum exceeded my hopes. I beg you not to cease to be unkind to them, and to push matters in this respect with all vigor imaginable.' It was in this cruelly oppressed city Elsevier attempted to sell scholarly books. He also attempted to publish books, and the dates they were issued tell the story of the effect of occupation. Until the city was occupied by the French nine works were issued. After the occupation only one work was published, in 1675, the joint venture of Pieter Elsevier and Hackius at Leyden, with whom Pieter was linked by marriage. In the same year Pieter closed the shop, selling the stock at public auction and even selling the shelving. Possibly there was not a great deal left to sell at auction. Graevius, an Utrecht professor with a European reputation, reporting to Nicolaas Heinsius on items Graevius purchased for Heinsius, remarked in his letter, 'There was almost nothing good in the bookseller's auction.' The act of holding an auction automatically barred Pieter from again engaging in bookselling in Utrecht. A gild regulation provided that members so disposing of book stocks must promise to quit the trade forever. Subsequently Pieter was a successful politician, being named to the town council of Utrecht on 17 December, 1677, magistrate on 17 October, 1678, and treasurer 20 November, 1678. In October, 1684, for an undiscovered reason, he was excluded from the Broad Council, and thus lost his place in the town oligarchy. He died in September, 1696.

The establishments at The Hague and Utrecht were, of course, subsidiary to the firm at Leyden, which continued to be for many years the chief Elsevier concern. The Leyden house attained its greatest fame under Bonaventura and Abraham Elsevier. Their story will be related in the following chapter, but important developments in the firm which should be noted occurred between the death of the founder and the forming of the famous partnership. After Louis Elsevier's death the business was carried on by his eldest son Mathijs, and his sixth son, Bonaventura. In 1617 Isaac, the son of Mathijs, founded independently the first printing business in the family; thus, after the death of Louis, there were two Leyden establishments: the brothers Mathijs and Bonaventura carried on their father's bookselling and publishing, and Isaac operated a printing house.

Mathijs had substituted for his father as beadle for a few months when his parent was absent in France and Germany. In 1607 the other beadle, Augustin Waersegger, died and Mathijs became a candidate for his place. He was recommended by none other than Joseph Juste Scaliger. Scaliger pointed out to the curators that Mathijs had a good knowledge of foreign languages, an important consideration in a university with many foreign students. 'I doubt,' he observed, 'whether there is anyone who could more fittingly discharge these functions or who is more worthy of being given an opportunity to do so than is Mathijs Elsevier,' and he added that Mathijs merited, because of his honesty, 'to be put in a position where he could provide for his family and make himself honorably useful to the University.' Three persons were nominated, Mathijs being the successful candidate. He continued in office until 1616 when he was dismissed for negligence in the matter of a fire at the University, but was reappointed the following year. He then held office until his death in 1640, his son-in-law, Petrus Caron, having been appointed to assist him in 1636 because of his advanced age.

His career as bookseller was short, for in September, 1622, being then about fifty-seven, he sold his interest in the business to his eldest son, Abraham, for eleven thousand two hundred and seventeen guilders: four thousand two hundred and seventeen guilders down, the balance at the rate of twelve hundred guilders per year. His brother Bonaventura and Abraham then formed the partnership which was to make the Elsevier name famous throughout Europe.

Isaac's printing establishment is important in the Elsevier story. This member of the family described himself as a printer in 1616 when he married Jacomina van Swieten, orphan daughter of an engineer who had lived at Leyden. Probably by using his wife's dowry he opened his own shop the following year. The first productions of the press in 1617 were financed by Isaac's grandfather, one of the first of them being by Dominicus Baudius on the twelve-year truce between Spain and the United Provinces.

After his grandfather's death Isaac printed books for his own establishment, for his father and uncle, and for other booksellers. As a consequence, Elsevier imprints of the period are varied: 'Printed by Isaac Elsevier,' 'At the shop of Isaac Elsevier,' 'For sale at the Elsevier Press,' and 'At the shop of Mathijs and Bonaventura Elsevier,' are common forms. Isaac opened the printing house when he was twenty and gave it up nine years later. Within that brief span he developed one of the best presses in Holland. The quality of work is evident in the large folio atlas which he printed for Jodocus Hondius, and the relative size of the establishment is indicated by the fact that it possessed six presses, whereas twenty-six years later there were nine printing houses in Leyden, three having four presses, five having two, and one single press establishment.

The most important step forward, both for Isaac and succeeding Elseviers, was his appointment as University Printer. On 7 February, 1620, the curators and burgomasters concluded to discharge Jan Paedts from office and to replace him with Isaac, in the meantime having theological theses printed by Jacob Marcus. The arrangement was concluded with both Elsevier and Marcus three days later. Isaac's instructions on taking the new post were much like those of his predecessors. He was to hold in readiness one and one-half presses for the printing of small tracts and pieces which the professors might want to use in their public lectures. Concerning longer works which professors wanted printed Elsevier would be obliged to print them if their publication were approved by the curators and the senate. If the works he was asked to print contained illustrations, these were to be furnished him with no cost to himself. On everything he printed he was obliged to state it had been printed by Isaac Elsevier,

official printer of the University of Leyden in Holland.
With regard to copy, all professors were to deliver theirs
to the printer complete, and the items were to be printed
in the order in which received; Elsevier was to furnish
good proof readers, and copy was not to be changed either
within the city of Leyden or elsewhere, by himself or
another, either directly or indirectly. One copy of every
book issued was to be placed by the printer in the University library. Elsevier was to bring from Frankfurt fair
at his own cost and peril all books desired by curators,
professors, and other notable members of the University,
and he was to be paid what other booksellers and printers
were reasonably paid for similar books. In all the work
which he produced during his term of office he was to
obey the laws of the Great Mighty States of Holland and
West Frisia, and the High and Mighty States General
of the United Netherlands. He was to take suitable oath
to perform what has been set forth, and for his pains was
to receive fifty guilders per year, a stipend raised five
years later to a hundred guilders.

After taking office Isaac exhibited the Elsevier characteristic of pressing his luck. A year after his appointment
he asked for a place in the University grounds. In the
petition the suppliant requested that, in order to accommodate and serve more ably professors and other members of
the University, he be allowed to live in his father's house
on the Rapenburg, near the gate of the University, since
the house was large and suitable for housing a press.
Elsevier pointed out that between the University gate
and his father's house there was a 'lost corner,' unat-
tractive, and not put to any use. In that corner of land he
proposed to erect a suitable gallery or building to use as a
retail store, thus having the convenient arrangement of a

retail book shop with printing plant behind it. The University, he pointed out, would by no means be hampered by the arrangement, but on the contrary, the grounds would be much improved, and, especially in cold and rainy weather, professors and students would find it a great convenience to take shelter in the book store, and theses could be better distributed from such a location. Moreover, as was well known, the University gate stood open from morning until evening, so that there was trouble from the boys and others who came and played ball in the open space. If a shop were there the University would be freed from the annoyance. The suppliant expressly stated that if the favor were granted he would never claim ownership of the land on which the building stood. The curators acceded to the request, stating the building was to be in accordance with the plan submitted, that it was to extend from the University wall to the wall of the botanic garden, and to be fourteen feet in width. Elsevier was to see to it that compositors and pressmen entered by the door to Mathijs' house, that is, the door opening on the street. The door of the new building opening into the University yard was to be reserved for students, professors, and suchlike people. He was to pay a yearly rent of eighteen guilders.

In 1625 an event occurred which placed the Elseviers in a firmer relationship with the University. A famous orientalist at the University, Thomas Erpenius, at great cost and labor, by buying types and having them cast, had gotten together an oriental press with Syriac, Chaldaic, Ethiopic, Arabic, Hebrew, and other letters. Being interested in oriental languages the University valued the types highly. * In the year mentioned, Erpenius having

* *The matrices were bought by Pieter van der Aa and are now the property of Enschedé in Haarlem*

died, the University negotiated to buy his books from his widow and also sought to have her promise not to sell the types outside Leyden. Eventually the bulk of the books was acquired for Cambridge, but the printing equipment was sold to Elsevier, an event noticed in faraway London. 'Since I wrote unto you last,' runs a letter from Bishop Usher to Samuel Ward dated 23 June, 1626, 'I have received intelligence from *Leyden* that all Erpenius's printed books are already sold; and his Matrices of the Oriental tongues are bought by Elsevier the Printer there . . .'

But having strengthened his position by purchasing oriental types, Isaac now showed himself one of the wayward Elseviers, and gave up the whole enterprise the following year. On 8 February, 1626, he wrote the curators and burgomasters to say that, 'Isaac Elsevier, official printer to the University, respectfully sets forth that he feels himself profoundly indebted to you, since you have been pleased to accord him favor, honor, and kindness in appointing him official printer of the University, a position which he has always endeavored to discharge as well as he could and which he would have desired to continue as long as possible, but because of the warlike troubles in Germany and in other places, the earnings of printers have fallen so low that he feels constrained to renounce it. He must transfer his printing equipment to his friends [his uncle Bonaventura and his cousin Abraham] who, being at the same time booksellers, will be able to take care of the duties more easily: for himself, he intends to embrace a new profession. He prays you will take it in good part, and he thanks you for the benevolence, honor, and favor with which you have overwhelmed him during these past years. He will always endeavor to show his gratitude and to repay you by doing for you all the services which his limited abilities permit.'

So ended Isaac's career in the book trades. Soon after (in March, 1626) he left Leyden and established himself at Rotterdam where he bought a tavern. Shortly before April, 1629, he forsook the innkeeper's calling to become provost general for the Admiralty of South Holland, Maas, and Waal; as such he had the rank of captain and was assisted in his duties by a lieutenant and four halberdiers. The rise in status can perhaps be partly explained by noting that his brother's father-in-law, Waesberghe, was printer to the Admiralty. In June, 1644, Isaac resigned his formidable office in favor of his brother Jacob and went to live in Wassenaar, a village situated midway between Leyden and The Hague. Later he and his two youngest sons were in the brewery business. He died at Cologne in 1651 on the way to visit his brother Jacob, who was then at Gensingen in the Palatinate. Isaac's act in turning over his printing business to his relatives gave to Bonaventura and Abraham control of both Elsevier enterprises, and they were in a fair way to create an outstanding establishment.

4

Abraham and Bonaventura Elsevier

THE partnership of Bonaventura and Abraham, formed in 1622, endured until 1652, Abraham devoting his attention to the actual printing while Bonaventura directed the enterprise. During the thirty-year period the men published nearly half the books issued by the Leyden Elseviers in the one hundred and thirty-two years of the firm's existence, and were easily the best typographers of the Elsevier dynasty. Their success was probably due to personal qualities, but external circumstances were in their favor. From the time the first Louis Elsevier arrived in Leyden in 1581 until the death of Bonaventura and Abraham in 1652, Leyden continued to increase in population and prosperity; but whereas before the time of Abraham and Bonaventura population growth, prices, and the cost of living shot up with great rapidity, during the period of the partnership the increases were less spectacular. This latter period of the city's growth, a period of peace and gradually expanding economy, was a more congenial climate for publishing. An illustration of changing conditions in Leyden is the fact that from 1581 to 1622, that is, from the arrival of Elseviers in the city to the formation of the Bonaventura and Abraham partnership, the Leyden population climbed from twelve thousand one hundred and forty-four to forty-four thousand seven hundred and forty-five, an increase of more than two hundred and sixty-eight per cent. During the period of the partnership population increased forty-one per cent, standing at about sixty-three thousand in 1652. The pre-Bonaventura and Abraham period covered, of course, a span of slightly more than forty years, whereas the partnership existed thirty years, so that it is not quite valid to compare the periods, but the difference in rates of increase, two hundred and sixty-eight per cent and forty-one per cent, are worth noting. The same deceleration is noticeable in the rate of price increases. Prices in the city of everyday necessities such as wheat, oats, rye, herring, beef, beans, cheese, butter, peat, soap, paper, and hay were sixty-three per cent higher in the years 1620 to 1624 than they had been in the years 1580 to 1584, whereas in the years 1650 to 1654 they had increased only thirty per cent over the years 1620 to 1624. One of the great scholars of Holland, Dr Nicolaas W. Posthumus, from whose works the statistics are taken, compiled a cost of living index, from which it appears the cost of living increased seventy-five per cent between the periods 1580 to 1584 and 1620 to 1624, whereas the increase from the years 1620 to 1624 to the years 1650 to 1654 was forty-three per cent. The same loss of momentum is evident in statistics for cloth production, the principal industry at Leyden. In 1584 the number of pieces of cloth of all varieties produced in the city was, in round figures, twenty-seven thousand, while in 1622 the figure was approximately ninety-nine thousand. After considerable fluctuation in the interim the figure for 1652 stood at eighty-two thousand pieces.

The general 'settling down' or consolidation was evident in the book industry, there being fewer printers and booksellers operating in the city in the second quarter of the seventeenth century than there had been in the first quarter, sixty-one being active in the first quarter century, whereas only fifty-five were in business at sometime during the second twenty-five year period. An accompaniment of slight diminution in numbers was better organization within the trade. Leyden was infested with intinerant peddlers who hawked books along the streets, a condition often found in university cities. In Groningen, as was noted in the previous chapter, urban booksellers complained to university officials about damage done them by interlopers who sold books in the town at public auction, thereby luring citizens, and especially students, to buy from them. It was explained that the interlopers demanded cash payment, which had the effect of making people slow in paying balances owed in town. The complainants also stated their prices were more reasonable than those of the itinerants, and that city booksellers sometimes waited a year or two or more for payment, and then perhaps did not receive it. In Leyden, Groningen, and other cities, it was found expedient to organize gilds of printers, publishers, and booksellers designed to control the market and prevent abuses in trade. Leyden booksellers and printers formed a gild in 1636, following the example of Middelburg bookmen who had formed an association in 1590, and Haarlem merchants who formed theirs in 1616. The Leyden gild was followed by one at Groningen in 1647.

But while the city and the book business were settling down to a period of orderly growth and quiet prosperity, the University, its fame having spread through the Continent, was entering the period of greatest expansion. Students flocked to it from all over Europe. The average number of new students per year for the years 1575 to

1600 was one hundred and five. For the quarter century 1601 to 1625, the annual new enrollment was two hundred and forty-nine, and for the second quarter of the century this average figure had jumped to four hundred and forty-three. The percentages of foreigners enrolling in the three periods were respectively thirty-seven per cent, forty-three per cent, and fifty-two per cent. Not only did enrollment increase greatly, but the latter years saw no diminution in the quality of faculty, activity in languages, classics, theology, medicine and law continuing with unabated energy.

Study of oriental languages, given great impetus by Thomas Erpenius, professor of Arabic and oriental languages from 1619 until his death in 1624, was carried forward with equal energy by his former student Jacobus Gool, or Golius. This professor of Arabic and oriental tongues in the years 1625 to 1667 was also, for most of the period, professor of mathematics, succeeding the famous Willebrordus Snellius (Snel van Royen). Golius mastered Arabic and Persian, was skilled in Turkish, and also studied Chinese. The same story was told of him that had been told about Erpenius, it being said that when he accompanied the Dutch ambassador to Morocco the Sultan was astonished at the purity of his Arabic. The duties of Erpenius as professor of Hebrew were taken over by Constantijn L'Empereur, who, during his sojourn at Leyden, was professor of Hebrew and Chaldaic languages, and also of theology.

The study of the classics continued with undiminished vigor. With the death of Scaliger the University lost its brightest jewel, but his place was taken by Claude Saumaise, or Salmasius, 'the second Scaliger,' and by Daniël Heinsius, student of Scaliger. Theology continued vital and creative. In the first quarter of the century the faculty had stirred up great questions; the disputes of Remonstrants, and Counter-Remonstrants, among others, had agitated the University and shaken it to its foundations. The theologians of the second quarter of the century also debated great problems, wrote books about them, published attacks and counter attacks, all to the great good of the book trades. Prominent among debates were those inspired by a Frenchman, René Descartes, who for a time lived near Leyden, where he struck up acquaintance with, and greatly influenced, a number of professors. The first man to introduce his dangerous thoughts into the University was François du Ban, professor of logic, ethics, and physics. Johannes van Wale, professor of medicine, and Frans van Schooten, the younger, sometime professor of mathematics, were his followers also; but his most ardent propagandist was Adrianus Heereboort, at various times professor of logic, philosophy, ethics, and politics. In 1647 this professor lectured in the University on the topic, 'The Freedom of Philosophic Thought,' declaring he believed 'it is necessary to renounce all of the idols of our spirit. We must rid ourselves of preconceived opinions and prejudices, and bring to the study of philosophy a virgin soul like that of the new born ... ' 'That,' continued the orator, 'was the approach of Aristotle and the most illustrious spirits of all the centuries and of all the nations, as it is in our day the approach of that incomparable genius, that unique master of the truth, rising out of shadows and servitude, René des Cartes.' The insidious progress of Cartesianism was opposed by the professors of theology, Jacobus Trigland and Adam Stuart; but the new philosophy so attracted students, Trigland complained, that whenever philosophical disputes were in progress in which the novelties were introduced, the students flew to them and theologians were left with few auditors. When Trigland attacked Cartesianism in a philosophical disputation, the occasion ended in tumult. Controversy became so serious that the rector proposed, among other remedial measures, that all pamphlets for or against Cartesianism be suppressed, that the teaching of metaphysics be temporarily discontinued, and that a general amnesty be proclaimed. While theologians debated with zest, and oriental and classical studies continued with full vigor, the schools of law and medicine lost none of their eminence, as indeed they did not for another hundred years.

On the one hand, then, there was a University growing physically and intellectually as no other university in the period was growing, and as it had not grown before, and on the other hand was a city which had passed the era of its most rapid growth and was undergoing quieter development. It is easy to find significance in irrelevant facts, but it does seem that the conditions described were those most favorable for the book business, and accounted in part for the great period of the Elseviers. The book business grows as education grows; war-torn cities and boom towns are not the most favorable locations for it. A city with fewer and better regulated book dealers assisted the Elseviers, and great intellectual activity likewise did so. An indication of how their business was affected by activity in the University is that with the exception of François du Ban, all men mentioned above as having a part in the Descartes controversy, Van Wale, Schooten, Heereboort, Trigland, and Adam Stuart, were published by them.

Although Bonaventura and Abraham had become partners in 1622 it was not until 1626 that they became official printers to the University. They did so on approximately the same conditions as had been accorded to previous University printers, it being stipulated, in fact, that they should have the position on the same terms as had been accorded their predecessor and relative, Isaac; that they should have the right to occupy the gallery or loggia which Isaac had built as a retail store in the University grounds; and that the oriental press which had been acquired from the widow of Thomas Erpenius should remain in the city at the service of the University. As an inducement in favor of their appointment, the Elseviers promised that if the office were awarded them, the oriental types would remain in Leyden for the use of the University; and that they would not permit their printing facilities to be diminished, but that they would in fact make them better and better to the honor and reputation of the University.

From the time they became University printers until 1651 they printed or published an average of eighteen works per year, the annual number sometimes being as low as eleven, and sometimes as high as twenty-three. As the years went by they published a larger proportion of their books in French. In the first five years as University printers the proportion of their books in French was about one per cent of the total; in the last five years a little better than fifty per cent were in French. They published many more books in Dutch than did their predecessors, and also printed volumes in Greek, Arabic, Italian, and German. As to subject, the works were those which would interest the educated world. At least fifteen publications were explicitly intended for textbooks, and of course many more were probably used in classes. Grammars of foreign languages are much in evidence on the list, there being French, Hebrew, Arabic, Spanish, Persian, and Greek grammars. The books in Italian include one first edition of Galileo, *Discorsi e dimostrazioni matematiche intorno à due nuove scienze attenenti alla mecanica & i movimenti locali del Signor Galileo Galilei* ... (1638), usually known in English as *Dialogue on Two New Sciences* ... In a dedicatory letter preceding the work Galileo remarks the Elseviers 'have done me the kindness to print this at their most excellent press.' Two other works by Galileo also were published by the Leyden firm.

A fair number of publications in French were plays, among them being: *Les Trois Dorotées*, *Le Virgile* of Scarron, four editions of *Le Cid*, by Corneille, three editions of his *Horace*, two editions each of his *Cinna*, *Le Menteur*, *La Suite du Menteur*, *La Mort de Pompée*, *Polyeucte*, and *Rodogune*, and also editions of *Héraclius*, the poem *D. Sanche d'Arragon*, and a collection of five Corneille plays. The fact that French plays were published by the Elseviers indicates the market the firm intended to supply. It has been observed that the masses of Dutch people preferred Spanish theatre, or imitations of it. Jonas A. van Praag found Dutch translations of plays by the Spanish writers Mira de Amescua, Jiménez de Enciso, Lope de Vega, Pérez de Montalván, Ruiz de Alarcón, Gaspar Aguilar, and Enríquez Gomez printed in the northern provinces, but none was printed by Elseviers. Wealthier classes developed, or attempted to develop, a taste for French theatre; they imported plays along with other French luxuries and refinements. French, not Spanish, playwrights were printed by Bonaventura and Abraham and other members of the family, indicating that the Elseviers aimed to be booksellers to the polite world.

That the partners printed so much of Corneille was due,

in part, to Constantijn Huygens, the friend of European talent and learning, who was much interested in the Elseviers. In February, 1644, he wrote from Paris to Bauterne to say, 'I am sending you a piece to show to their highnesses, *The Death of Pompey* by Corneille, which surpasses, they say, all that he has done before. In short, *The Cid* has never gained such a reputation. If, after the higher powers have been satisfied, you wish to turn it over to the Elseviers, I feel sure that they will be very glad to have it, for they have no hatred of gain.' It thus happened that in the same year the play was published at Paris it was also published by the Elseviers at Leyden. The partners also originated a profitable line when they published their 'Republics,' little volumes which continued to be printed by their successors and which were widely imitated. It has been suggested that because so many nationalities were represented in the student body at Leyden, interest in foreign cities and countries was greatly stimulated. The 'Republics' were published to satisfy the interest. Usually they contained an account of a country's topography, history, system of government, chief statesmen, the court, and the ruling house. Sometimes statistics on state revenue, expenditures, population, and the army were given. The volume on the Empire of the Grand Mogul, for example, contains data on the topography, climate, soil, customs, superstitions, government, money, weights and measures, size of the army, and history of India. The one on China, in addition to a description of Chinese government, lands and beliefs, gives an account of the travels of Marco Polo and of Bento de Goes in China. The content varied from volume to volume, some volumes being written for the series while others were adapted to it. The book on Africa was the famous work by Jean Leon, originally written in Arabic, translated into Italian at the request of Pope Leo X, retranslated into Latin, and so printed several times before the Elseviers issued it with the title *Ioannis Leonis Africani Africae descriptio IX lib. absoluta*. The *Sabaudiae Respublica* was a simplified version of an historical treatise of Lambert van der Burch. On the other hand, De Laet, an Elsevier employee whose work is well known to American historians, produced a number of volumes to order. The first volume he worked on was that on England, issued in 1625, mainly a translation of a work by Sir Thomas Smith but also containing material contributed by De Laet. He also finished the volume on Italy begun by Thomas Segeth, and then compiled volumes on Spain, France, The Netherlands, India, Persia, Portugal, Poland-Lithuania-Prussia-Livonia, and Turkey. Beginning in 1625 with the account of England, the Elseviers printed thirty-five different Republics, ending with the one on Japan which appeared in 1649. Strictly speaking, not all volumes were descriptions of countries. In 1633 a volume appeared made up of Hugo Grotius' *De mari libero* and Paulus Merula's *De Maribus*. The little books were so successful that other printers copied them, and there were about as many 'Republics' issued by others during the lifetime of the partners as there were issued by Elseviers. These descriptions of strange lands and cities have been called guidebooks, predecessors of Baedekers, but they could hardly have been intended for the purpose. Being in Latin they were not in a convenient form for large classes of travelers: merchants, seamen, and soldiers. The claim for the books ought to be that together they formed the first inexpensive series; as such they were the fore-runners of the 'Chronicles of America,' the 'World

Classics,' and similar inexpensive sets. The partners also instituted a series of cheap duodecimo editions of classics, which, damned by some and praised by others, proved highly successful.

Probably the great claim of the press to distinction, in the eyes of both Elseviers and University, was that it was equipped to print oriental languages. The University's regard for this phase of printing is apparent in two actions taken by the curators. In February, 1627, they resolved that eight common printers and journeymen compositors in oriental languages employed at the University press should henceforth enjoy freedom from excise and imposts as did other common members of the University. Practically, this meant the beer of oriental compositors was tax free, no small advantage for a printer. Later (in 1630) it was resolved that any typefounder who could produce oriental types, who chose to reside at Leyden, and who enrolled in the University should also enjoy freedom from imposts on wine and beer. The maintenance of an oriental press was probably more expensive than either University or printers at first had appreciated. In August, 1631, Bonaventura, appearing before the curators, complained of the great cost of the press, especially the expense of proofreaders for oriental languages, and requested a reasonable subsidy be granted his firm. In later years whenever the printers petitioned for an increase in stipend they pointed to the cost of maintaining the oriental equipment.

As a matter of fact, difficulties about money which now developed between printers and University were due only partly and secondarily to the cost of printing with oriental types. The primary cause was both printers and University were on the rack of rising prices. Two years after their appointment the printers petitioned to have their stipend increased, and in February, 1628, the curators acceded to the request, granting them two hundred guilders yearly in place of the hundred formerly received. Nearly four years later (November, 1631), as a result of the complaint of Bonaventura previously noted, the stipend was raised to three hundred guilders. In 1649, University finances being somewhat strained, it was resolved to consider abolishing the annual retainer paid the Elseviers, and in spite of the printers' protests the emolument was actually discontinued in February, 1650. A year later the printers requested that the retainer not only be reinstated but increased. The curators resolved to postpone consideration of the petition. There then ensued a long conflict between press and University, the Elseviers endeavoring to have the stipend reinstated, the curators making an effort to avoid payment. Long after Bonaventura and Abraham were in their graves the curators, by an infinite variety of postponements, further considerations, and further investigations, avoided giving a direct answer to the perennial Elsevier request for a salary.

Printing for the University was only one aspect of the Elsevier business. They printed, of course, trade books on their own account; maintained their retail book store inside the University grounds; and held book auctions fairly frequently. Probably most auction records have disappeared, but their catalogues for auctions of the libraries of Professor Reinier de Bondt, François Rave-linghen, Johan Rutgers (who had died at The Hague), Franciscus Gomarus, Lodewijk de Dieu, and for a number of others are extant. Possibly their auctioneering and trafficking with students were causes for Leyden booksellers drawing up (in February, 1633) a petition addressed to the city government, and submitted for consideration by the University. The petitioners complained that because of disorder in the book trade their livelihood was greatly diminished. As a consequence, they asked, first, that henceforth no bookseller be allowed to hold auctions unless he were quitting business, although the heirs of a deceased bookseller might auction his stock; second, that only the libraries of those who died in and around the city should be sold at auction, and that libraries should not be brought from other places; third, that booksellers should not buy books from students, who in some cases owed other booksellers for the material they were selling; fourth, books should not be sold from house to house; and finally, that there should be no pirating of works printed by others.

Since their advice was asked, the rector and senate pointed out that it was advantageous to University members to have libraries brought to Leyden and auctioned, for they thus got books difficult to find. They objected to prohibiting students from selling books to booksellers since, as they pointed out, students brought books from the lower schools which they might want to sell, and also as time went on, some books were of no further use to them. Regarding piracy, the learned gentlemen pointed out that booksellers were taking away their own freedom to reprint profitable books issued in other cities, and what the booksellers desired would make it possible for dealers elsewhere to pirate books published by the University of Leyden although printers in the city could not do so. It is not difficult to see how the Elseviers were concerned in the questions. They held auctions of scholars' libraries brought from other parts of Holland; having a shop within the

University grounds they were in the best position to buy books from students; and as University printers they had no desire to see their own works pirated without having the right to a little piracy on their own account. The views expressed by the University authorities would be the views of the Elseviers, and there may have been collaboration between them in framing the reply. A compromise was reached endeavoring to embody the views of both booksellers and University, but since the views were so disparate, the compromise was weak and cumbersome.

There are considerably more data available on relations of the Elseviers with individual scholars than there are for their relations with booksellers and the University. About half of those who were Leyden professors during the time the Elseviers served edited or wrote books published by them. Generally these men respected, but did not admire, the publishers, since their avariciousness made admiration difficult. Johannes F. Gronovius, sometime a Leyden professor, complained he was charged fifteen *stuivers* by the Elseviers for delivering a letter written to him by Selden, the author of *Mare Clausum*. The charge was made although the letter was contained in a package forwarded to the Elseviers, and there was no expense involved in delivering it. This, observed Gronovius, was the reward for all the pains he had taken to edit Seneca for them. The printers gave even more interesting evidence of regard for a penny. A few years after complaining of the charge on the Selden letter, Gronovius received through the Elseviers an incunabulum edition of Livy, sent to him by Nicolaas Heinsius. He was charged by the printers for transporting the volume, even though he was editing Livy for them at the time, and needed the book in his editorial work. He complained that, 'As if it were not enough that I furnish them such work free, they go further and confer upon me a certain amount of expense. But,' he concluded, 'there is no use trying to whiten a Negro.' Later he wrote a fatherly piece of advice to a friend who considered having a book printed by the Elseviers. 'If you have dealings with these printers,' he advised, 'be careful not to follow my example. I am too accommodating, and they have treated me as they pleased. The Elseviers have given me twelve copies of the Livy and of the Seneca, and twenty of the notes. That is all the profit I have gotten from my labor. Furthermore, I have had to pay one hundred and fifty guilders for the copies of the first which I have given away, and a little less for the other. There you have the liberality of these fellows.' A more fair-minded man and family friend of the Elseviers was Nicolaas Heinsius; yet even Heinsius, in writing to Gronovius on behalf of the Elseviers urging him to finish a preface, added, 'With regard to the dedication, it appears that, misers that they are, they want to conserve the right of making that themselves.' It will be remembered, of course, that in those days the person to whom a book was dedicated usually paid a little ready money for the flattery. There are other stories of Elsevierian avarice; the worst aspersions were cast by Lucas Holstenius, and concerned the geographer, Cluver, whose works were printed by the Elseviers many times. Cluver died in 1623, and his wife having died before him, his mother-in-law took his orphaned children and departed for London. She had only enough money to subsist for a few months, but it appears the Elseviers promised to procure at least the necessities for her. The slender resources of the family were soon exhausted. The woman wrote the Elseviers for help, but they never replied, and the pitiful unfortunates in an alien land were soon without food and fuel. The little girl fell ill and died; her brother was soon down with pneumonia, complicated by ulceration of the arms and chest. Holstenius came upon the family in this condition. He bent all his efforts to help and succeeded in getting money for them; but this was not an incident to arouse admiration for the printer-booksellers.

While avarice was the most serious blemish on their personal characters, the most serious criticism of their work as publishers was that they were too much under the influence of Daniël Heinsius. The Heinsius family, like the Elseviers, were refugees from the southern Netherlands. Daniël had studied at Leyden, where he was Scaliger's favorite student. Subsequently he was University librarian, and at various times, professor of Greek, poetry, politics, and history. The verdict of classicists is that as a scholar he was not above average; but his reputation did not depend only on scholarship. He wrote Latin prose, and both Dutch and Latin poetry. He had a sufficient knowledge of oriental languages, was a tremendous worker, intolerably sensitive, and as proud as Lucifer. Because both families were refugees, and because as University librarian he bought books from, and had books bound by Elseviers, he knew them intimately, and acquired ascendancy over them which resulted in his being practically editor of their press. His influence began with the original Louis Elsevier, but was strongest during the regime of Bonaventura and Abraham. These men were not university graduates, and, engaged as they were in printing and selling scholarly books, they stood in need of precisely such guidance as Heinsius supplied; but accepting it had its drawbacks. A poor scholar who had the misfortune to wound the delicate sensibilities of the great man had small chance of being published by Elseviers. Since Heinsius' feelings were injured with little effort the Elsevier list was unduly restricted. Among Heinsius' numerous enemies there was, for example, the German, Jacob Gebhardt, a thoroughly competent scholar, who had taught at Heidelberg, in Sweden, and in the last years of his life at Groningen. In 1617 he edited Catullus, Tibullus, and Propertius, and sent the manuscripts off to Heinsius, seeking his influence in having the Elseviers publish them. But they were not published; in spite of entreaties they were not returned to him; and, in fact, he never saw the manuscripts again. About 1628 Gebhardt edited and annotated the texts of Quintus Curtius and Cornelius Nepos. Bonaventura and Abraham agreed to print them, but later, after they talked the matter over with Heinsius, Gebhardt suspected, they decided to postpone the undertaking. Four years later the work was still in manuscript. Gebhardt complained bitterly that Heinsius hated the Germans and as a consequence blocked the project. 'He thinks the Flemish are the only educated people,' Gebhardt complained, 'and no one knows how to write except himself. The foolish adulations of our people have turned his head.' Another gentleman to feel the malice of Heinsius was Jean Louis Guez *sieur* de Balzac. He was perhaps not a profound scholar, but certainly a popular, influential writer, and an elaborately courteous man. On one occasion he presumed to level some criticisms at Heinsius' tragedy, *Herod, the Infanticide*, and received a verbal lashing from the author in return. 'Not to say worse of that great adversary,' Balzac wrote of Heinsius, 'he has taken my good intentions the wrong way; he has not received my civilities as they ought to

have been received. I have had only the intention of
giving him some material to amuse him; I spoke to him
with all kinds of deference; I asked him for instruction on
several points of his tragedy, *Herod, the Infanticide*. Those
were my actions. But he on the contrary did not wish to
receive my civilities and shies away from my compliments.
I asked for instruction from him, and he throws rocks at
me.'

But more than all others, Claude Saumaise aroused the
antagonism of Heinsius. An unfortunate quarrel developed between the two men out of which the Elseviers
were able to make a few more or less honest guilders.
When the great philologist, Saumaise, came to Leyden
bearing the reputation of 'The Second Scaliger,' he
unconsciously trod on important toes, since Heinsius, the
favorite of Scaliger, could fittingly claim such a sobriquet.
In addition to the difficulty of having acquired more
fame as a scholar than was appropriate, Saumaise was
cursed with a Gallic wit. There is a story attributed to
him, perhaps apocryphal, that he described Holland as a
country where all the four elements were worth nothing
and where the demon of gold, crowned with tobacco, was
seated on a throne of cheese. On one occasion, Heinsius
observed that if the works of Saumaise and himself were
placed in one pan of a balance and the works of all other
scholars were placed in the other pan, the two pans would
be in equilibrium. Saumaise replied that the same result
would obtain if Heinsius' works were added to those in the
other pan. Between the two men, the one talented, intelligent, envious, and malicious, the other immensely
learned, proud, and witty, a great hostility developed.
Saumaise, 'the honor of the University,' as Dudley Car-
leton called him, arrived in Leyden in 1632. In 1634 he

wrote Pierre Dupuy to say, 'The Elseviers who are the best printers here are in the power of you know who, and they only work for those of whom he approves. He has prevented them until now from doing anything for me.' It was not until 1638 that the University printers issued a book by him. In that year he paid his respects to the great commercial state wherein he resided by publishing *De Usuris,* in which he brought his great learning to bear on the question of putting money out to interest, and justified it on religious and ethical grounds. He complained that the publishing process proceeded slowly, 'Because,' he said, 'the printer is the pensioner and dependant of my antagonist.' The dislike smoldering between the two men burst into flame anew during the Guez de Balzac-Heinsius controversy, which has been alluded to. Balzac published a *Discourse on the tragedy of Mr Heinsius entitled, 'Herod, the Infanticide,'* (1636). Heinsius replied immediately with a *Letter . . . which Answers the Dissertation of Mr Balzac on 'Herod, the Infanticide.'* Saumaise, unable finally to keep out of so attractive a quarrel, took Balzac's part by writing in 1644, *A Letter by Claude Saumaise to Gilles Ménage concerning Heinsius' Tragedy 'Herod, the Infanticide' and Balzac's criticism of it.* For some years the University had endeavored to bring about peace between the antagonists. Following this battle in printer's ink, a peace treaty was signed at last, Heinsius agreeing to use his influence to prevent his friend Schoockius publishing a book against Saumaise, and the latter on his part agreeing to suppress his *Letter to Ménage,* mentioned above. The book had already been published at Paris, and the University curators commissioned the Elseviers to go to Paris and buy the unsold portion of the edition. Bonaventura sent Johannes, the son of his partner Abraham, to execute the task. Johannes bought the remaining copies, about three hundred, for which the curators reimbursed him to the amount of two hundred and twenty-five guilders. Notwithstanding the efforts of the curators to suppress the book, Heinsius complained it was still possible to buy it under the counter at the Elseviers.

There is a perceptible pattern in Heinsius' malevolence. He was a strict Calvinist and an anti-Arminian, having been secretary of the Synod of Dordrecht. Abraham and Bonaventura were also orthodox Calvinists, whereas some who complained of the bad treatment at the hands of Heinsius and the Elseviers were Arminians. Hugo Grotius and Gerardus Vossius had both suffered for their Arminianism. In 1638 Grotius, then at Paris, wrote to ask the advice of Vossius on a possible publisher for his book. Vossius replied that 'No one would be better suited to publish your works than the Elseviers. They excel all other printers in the quality of their paper and the beauty of their types. I don't think that they would refuse to print the work if they were not dissuaded from doing it by certain people, and above all by one who calls himself your friend ... Envy and malice have become second nature to him. These qualities are evident in his actions toward all who have talent and character. I have had the sad experience of them myself. Meursius felt them, and the Great Saumaise in his turn felt them also ... ' Grotius replied that 'There is no use thinking about the Elseviers because of the man who reigns over their house like a sovereign, that man who hates me and whose letters I have let go unanswered because he has long treated mine the same way, a man spoiled by fortune ... ' Their orthodoxy may also have made the Elseviers unenthusiastic about Descartes, and caused them to miss the opportunity to print his *Discourse on Method*. That Descartes wanted the Elseviers to print his work is evident from a letter written by him to Constantijn Huygens in October, 1635. With the idea in mind he went to Leyden the following year, but the Elseviers, he said, who had given evidence previously of wanting to be the publishers, 'imagining, I think, that I would not escape them when they saw me here have shown a desire to be coaxed or persuaded.' Accordingly Descartes entrusted the manuscript to Jan Maire, another Leyden printer. There is no direct evidence the Elseviers acted cavalierly toward Descartes because of their orthodoxy, but it appears this might have been a factor.

In addition to trafficking with scholars, printing and selling books, and discharging their obligations to the University, the partners busied themselves with extramural trade. They continued to attend the Frankfurt book fair, and after 1637, when Jacob Elsevier retired, they managed the two bookstalls in the Great Hall at The Hague. Since 1632 they had sent agents to sell books in Copenhagen. This Danish book trade was one result of the Thirty Years' War. Before the outbreak of war in 1618 Danish booksellers had replenished their stocks at the Frankfurt fair, but the war made the journey unprofitable. The Dutch then exploited the Danish book market by taking book stocks to Denmark. The trade proved attractive and profitable, so much so that Danish booksellers in 1624 complained that foreign merchants in Denmark prolonged their stay there beyond all measure. Louis Elsevier, the third of the name and a nephew of Bonaventura, visited Copenhagen on behalf of the Leyden firm in 1632; he returned again in 1634 and in 1637, and he was followed in his job of traveling agent by an employ-

ee, Nicolaas Schouten. After Schouten, Johannes and
Daniël Elsevier visited Copenhagen. In 1619 to 1640
King Christian IV constructed a bourse in the city. In the
hall of the bourse were thirty-six stalls or shops, and both
Elseviers and the Janszoon firm of Amsterdam rented
space for bookshops there. It is probable that the Elsevier
Copenhagen branch was maintained until the death of
the partners in 1652. Bonaventura and Abraham also
did business in Sweden, and Queen Christina endeavored
to induce them to establish a branch in that country also.
One of our own printers who acquired some fame during
the eighteenth century admonished us that if we were
diligent in business we would stand before kings. These
Elseviers were diligent in business, and were sought by a
queen.

Bonaventura and Abraham exhibit a striking combi-
nation of good and bad qualities. There is no gainsaying
that whenever a contemporary remarked on their personal
characteristics, the chances were it was an unflattering
remark. It is equally true that whenever their work was
spoken of it was usually with high praise. Stingy, un-
scrupulous, as they appeared to be in business matters,
they showed idealism, devotion, and careful effort when
producing books. 'They were,' says Willems, 'devoted to
their art. From the outset they aimed at typographic
perfection ... Never were printers imbued as were they
with a conception of the dignity and pre-eminent importance of their profession. They returned with pleasure
to that theme in the notices placed at the head of their
publications, and each time in terms marked with a
grave dignity which commands respect. They were proud
of their labor, and made it their glory.' Excellent typography was an accomplishment appreciated in their day

74

as it is in ours; perhaps more, for when Abraham died in 1652 the University honored the memory of his skill and devotion to his craft by striking a medal in his honor. Abraham's partner, Bonaventura, died a few months later. They had between them brought the Leyden firm to the apogee of its fame, their successors never equaling their accomplishments.

5

The Successors to Abraham and Bonaventura Elsevier

THE Leyden firm endured sixty years after the deaths of Bonaventura and Abraham in 1652. During that period it was operated first by Johannes and Daniël Elsevier, the sons of Abraham and Bonaventura respectively; then by Johannes alone; then successively by Johannes' widow and his son Abraham. The story of the later Elseviers is one of declining activity and prestige. It is perhaps natural this should be so. The firm was a family business; in 1652 it was already more than seventy years old. Although some joint stock companies, such as the Hudson's Bay Company or the Peninsular and Oriental, may appear indestructible, family concerns of such an age are frequently on the decline. This is one explanation for the waning fortunes of the firm, but probably other reasons are to be found in prevailing economic and political conditions. The Dutch sometimes say the second half of the seventeenth century was the era of their greatest wealth and power, the time when they stood highest among nations; but eminence and wealth aroused envy. By the Navigation Act of 1651 the British Commonwealth sought to break the Dutch hold on the carrying trade, and in the war that resulted (1652–4), although the Dutch achieved great things under brilliant admirals, Witte de With, Tromp and de Ruyter, they came close to disaster. In a second war with Britain in 1665–7 they swept the English from the seas and, indeed, swept the English channel itself, a humiliation which caused Mr Pepys, the navy's surveyor-general of the victualling office, to write that, 'All our hearts do now ake; for the newes is true that the Dutch have broke the chaine [blocking the seaway] and burned our ships, and particularly *The Royal Charles*.' Pepys confessed that with the Dutch roaming freely in the channel, 'I am left alone here at the office; and the truth is, I am glad my station is to be here, near my own home and out of danger . . . '

Dutch prosperity also aroused enmity and fear in the French. Colbert, Louis XIV's great minister, spoke of Holland as the most powerful republic since the Roman Empire, and believed the principal object of the Dutch was 'to acquire the trade of the whole world into their own hands . . . and to rob other nations of the same.' It was clear to him that, 'upon this they base the principal doctrine of their government, knowing full well that if they but have the mastery of trade, their power will continually wax on land and sea and will make them so mighty that they will be able to set up as arbiters of peace and war in Europe and set bounds at their pleasure to the justice and all the plans of princes.'

In 1672 the English, French, and two subsidiary vultures, the Bishop of Munster and the Archbishop-Elector of Cologne and Liège, made a concerted effort to crush the Netherlands. The war was a catastrophe for the Republic, and but for poor judgment by the French commander at a critical moment when he might have passed the water barrier, the Dutch would have been overrun and utterly defeated. But they were sustained by the courage of their leaders, De Witt, the Grand Pensionary, and the Prince of Orange, who declared he 'would rather be hewn to pieces,' than accept such terms of peace as the English and French offered him. His determination was justified, for in the following year, 1673, the French withdrew from practically all Dutch territory. In the latter half of the century, then, in addition to other wars, the Dutch successfully defended themselves against the combined efforts of the most powerful navies and armies in Europe. But even as they appeared to be at the pinnacle of their success and power certain facts presaged somber and difficult times ahead. The commerce of the Dutch did not continue to expand as rapidly as heretofore, while the commerce of their rivals, principally England, expanded at an increasing rate. Business was not as good as it had been; more capital was available than could be usefully employed in Dutch commerce and industry. Extravagant and Frenchified habits were more prevalent, and the gulf between the mass of citizenry and the ruling class widened. Overseas the Dutch were often forced upon the defensive. In 1654 their last stronghold in Brazil, which had seemed likely to become a Dutch dominion, fell into the hands of the Portuguese, although it was not until 1661 the treaty was signed returning Brazil to the Portuguese in consideration of eight million guilders. In the same year the Formosa settlements were lost to the Chinese, and in 1664 New York for the first time came under English rule. These few disquieting statements can be made about Holland in the latter half of the seventeenth century, ominous for the future of Holland perhaps, but not necessarily for a publishing house.

Turning from the country as a whole to the city of Leyden, a statistic worth noting is the number of pieces of

SUCCESSORS TO ABRAHAM AND BONAVENTURA

cloth produced annually, for textiles were the city's basic industry. In 1652 production stood at eighty-two thousand pieces, and in general increased gradually until 1664. In that year Colbert imposed a tariff on Dutch cloth, and Leyden was stricken with the plague. The following year the English war broke out, enduring until 1667, when Colbert imposed a second punitive tariff. As a result not only did the industry fail to expand, but production for the four years from 1664 to 1667 actually fell off about five per cent from the figure for the previous four years. Following these misfortunes, production rose steadily to one hundred and thirty-eight thousand pieces in 1671; but the following year was one of disastrous war; only one hundred and ten thousand pieces were produced, and by 1678 the number fell to about eighty-five thousand. The industry never again revived. When the last Elsevier engaged in printing died in 1712, production stood at fifty-five thousand, eight hundred and thirty-two pieces. Not only did production decline, but prices for goods declined over the period also, so that loss of prosperity was greater than production statistics indicate. The stagnation in industry was reflected in the city's population. In 1652, when Bonaventura and Abraham died, there were about sixty-three thousand inhabitants; when their descendant, Abraham, died in 1712, the population was about fifty-one thousand. From Dr Posthumus' index it is apparent the cost of living was down twelve per cent in the period 1710 to 1714 from what it had been in 1650 to 1654. Obviously it is not true that the fortunes of later Elseviers *exactly* paralleled economic prosperity in Leyden; but it is at least true over the period discussed that prosperity of both Elseviers and the city markedly declined.

Paradoxically, while the basic industry and the Else-vier firm were declining, book trades as a whole were prospering. The Netherlands were becoming the book center of Europe, and in this, the second half of the century, the number of printers and booksellers in Leyden increased fifty-eight per cent over what it had been in the first half of the century. Other Dutch cities experienced similar increases in printing and book trades, the number of printers and booksellers operating in Amsterdam in the latter half of the century being four hundred and sixty-three as compared with two hundred and fifty in the first half. But the character of the business was changed. Political pamphlets, called 'blue books,' appeared in increasing numbers. The most astounding period for them was the year 1672, when a contemporary wrote, 'The blue books flew in masses through the land'; and the historian, Dr Gustaaf J. Renier, estimates about as many pamphlets appeared in that year as had appeared in the previous three-quarters of a century. Also striking was the increasing number of books in Dutch. Statistics on publishing for the era are not too reliable, but it appears that of books selling for more than a guilder, an ever increasing proportion were in Dutch, the number in that language in the second half of the century being nearly three times the number published in the first half. Publications selling for less than a guilder would be pamphlets and ephemera which were preponderately in Dutch. As a concomitant, production of books in Latin was perhaps twenty-nine per cent less in the last half of the century than the figure at which it had stood in the first half. From about 1650, also, the number of books in French greatly increased, thanks to the cultivation of a taste for French literature, to the almost complete freedom of the press, and to increasing restrictions on the press in France. The book business was, then, quite a different affair from what it had been in the days of Louis Elsevier. Bonaventura and Abraham sensed the change and conformed to it. In the last five years of operation, as has been noted in the preceding chapter, a little more than fifty per cent of books printed by them were in French. But their successors did not realize the importance of the change and did not follow the lead given them. This fact will become apparent in the account of the later Elseviers which follows. The latter members of the firm found themselves in a period of transition, an especially precarious period, when other industries were declining, when the book business, as it had existed, was retrograding, but when new possibilities in the commerce of books were unfolding. It was a time for those in that commerce to be vigilant and imaginative in the conduct of business.

It has been found useful, also, in attempting to explain Elsevier fortunes, to look at the status of the University with which they were connected. In the previous chapter it was indicated the second quarter of the century, roughly the period from 1626 to 1650, was the era of great expansion for the University. Within those years eleven thousand seventy-six students registered, fifty-two per cent of whom came from outside the Netherlands or its colonies. In the succeeding twenty-five years the number decreased and the student body became more parochial, nine thousand nine hundred and forty enrolling in the years from 1651 to 1675, slightly less than thirty-six per cent of whom came from outside the Netherlands or its dependencies. In the next quarter century the new matriculants further declined to eight thousand one hundred and eight, and in the first quarter of the eighteenth century to six thousand seven hundred and twenty-two, the proportions of foreigners being forty-four per cent and forty-one per cent respectively. Great names also disappeared from the faculty. Daniël Heinsius died in 1655, L'Empereur in 1648, Salmasius in 1653, Du Ban in 1643, Golius in 1667. There were splendid men on the Leyden faculty after the first half of the seventeenth century but possibly the body as a whole never again stood so high in the opinion of its contemporaries as it did in that era. The University which later Elseviers dealt with lacked the brilliance of the institution their forbears had served.

In 1652 Abraham and Bonaventura passed on their business to their respective sons, Johannes and Daniël, the latter being twenty-six and the former thirty when they succeeded their parents in the Leyden concern. Both had been well prepared for their vocations. In 1638, when he was sixteen, Johannes had been sent to live with the printer Guillaume Pelé in Paris, where, in addition to increasing his knowledge of printing, he learned the intricacies of the French book trade and became acquainted with French bibliophiles and scholars. He remained at Paris until 1640 and then returned to Leyden, entering the University as a student in philosophy. But the next year he was evidently back in Paris, for a regulation of Parisian printers and booksellers for that year read, 'The syndics and inspectors of the book trade have obtained at their request a sentence from the civil lieutenant, 27 April, 1641, by which he is called upon to have Elsevier close his shop [at the fair?] three weeks after he has unpacked his merchandise, and to forbid Elsevier to sell any books bound or in sheets except to booksellers, which is according to the regulations, upon pain of a fine of one hundred pounds and confiscation of his goods without further process.' Johannes also visited Sorø, Denmark, on business in 1643, was back at Paris in 1644, and stayed in the city from October 1645 until February 1646. It is apparent also that he took some part in direction of the business at Leyden before his father died.

His partner, Daniël, received a similar education. He spent two and a half years with the Parisian bookseller Pierre Le Petit at the Sign of the Golden Fleece, returned to enroll at the University of Leyden, and then set out on travels for the firm, among other journeys visiting Stockholm with Nicolaas Heinsius in 1650. The young men, then, had good training and experience, but the firm they formed lacked imagination and versatility. Their fathers, sensing a changing market, had printed, in their last five years, more than half their books in French. The young partners in their first two full years of operation (1653 and 1654) printed forty-one volumes, a production rate about equal their predecessors' in their best years, but they relied heavily on classic languages, printing only twenty-seven per cent of their books in French. Not only that, they failed to break new ground; about twenty-seven per cent of the books they published were new editions or reissues of works already published by preceding Elseviers.

Inevitably the partners were tendered the office of University printer, but they showed remarkable lack of enthusiasm about accepting it. Their fathers had pleaded in vain to have restored the three hundred guilder annual stipend formerly accorded the printer. In February, 1653, before accepting the position, Johannes and Daniël also sought to have it reinstated, declaring the burden of maintaining the oriental press was so great they could not undertake the office.

Confronted with a minor rebellion, the curators pondered the matter and agreed that Golius, professor of Arabic, should formulate fair conditions on which the oriental press could be operated. To make it profitable for the printers, Golius recommended, among other things, that they be authorized to print sixty or eighty signatures in oriental languages in a year for the University, and that they be allowed to have a voice in the choice of material they were to print in order that material likely to bring a profit might be published. But the heart of the matter was the question of an annual retainer, and Golius' proposals let it severely alone. In June of the same year the curators decided to attempt to have the young men continue the oriental press for five or six years on the old terms. If this could not be done, they concluded somewhat irrelevantly to negotiate with one of the other leading printers to purchase the oriental press, if the Elseviers should sell it, and arrange with the printer in question to operate it for the University. The representatives of the curators were also to discuss with the hypothetical purchaser of the oriental equipment the terms on which he would accept the duties of official printer to the University. The scheme was ingenious but unfortunately the Elseviers did not offer to sell, and in August the curators yielded, contracting with Johannes and Daniël to undertake the office in consideration of a yearly stipend of three hundred guilders. As an added inducement, both they and their foreman were to be free of tax on wine and beer, as were other members of the University. They were to furnish a copy of each book printed by them to the University, were to supply the

University and library with unbound books at the same discount rate they allowed other booksellers, and were to print sixty or seventy leaves in the oriental tongues each year. Other conditions of the agreement were, in general, those which had been tendered to University printers from the beginning; that is, they were to print on good paper with good types, were, with some possible exceptions, to style themselves in the imprint, 'Official printers to the University of Leyden in Holland,' were to bring necessary books from the Frankfurt fair, and so forth. There is nothing remarkable in the further relations between printers and University. In February, 1655, the curators protested against an exorbitant printing bill, but the context of the protest makes apparent the alleged overcharge could easily have been due to neglect of University administrators to make clear what could be printed at University expense.

It was remarked the firm of Johannes and Daniël appeared to lack vitality and versatility. Since Daniël became, in later years, the most successful and personable of Elsevier bookmen, the faults may be laid to Johannes. It is possible, even probable, Daniël saw the shortcomings in the firm's activities. Possibly also he was irked by the temperament of his cousin, who repeatedly drew up grand designs which were never executed. In any event, he left Leyden and in May, 1655, entered the firm of his cousin Louis Elsevier, bookseller and publisher at Amsterdam. The ostensible, and perhaps real, reason for the change was that he had married Anna Beerninck, granddaughter of his Uncle Joost and ward of his cousin Louis. Daniël's departure left Johannes to carry the Leyden business alone, and he was without such tutelage as Daniël Heinsius had rendered his predecessors. Nicolaas, the son of Heinsius, had given promise of being to later Elseviers what Daniël had been to earlier members of the family, but Johannes had alienated his interest. In 1651, while Abraham and Bonaventura were still living, Johannes contracted to publish the Latin poems of Nicolaas Heinsius, but when he discovered they contained sly digs at Saumaise he delayed publication until after the death of that scholar in 1653. The tactic aroused Heinsius' indignation. 'Better than anyone,' he wrote an Elsevier relative at The Hague, 'you know all the Elseviers owe to my father. The memory of his benefactions ought always to be with them; but far from that, they have not scrupled to print odious libels by that scoundrel Saumaise who sought to dishonor my father and myself ... When we have complained they have professed to be simple printers, without knowledge of letters, intent simply on making a profit, without responsibility for what was printed. But if, in our turn, we attacked Saumaise, they assumed the prerogatives of editors. From this you may judge of their good faith. .. ' The result of Johannes' action was that Nicolaas transferred his interest and affections to the Amsterdam Elseviers.

It is worth noting that Johannes endeavored to compensate for his lack of interest in bookselling and his need for guidance in publishing. In view of the contemplated departure of his partner, Daniël, in May, 1654, he contracted with one Charles Gerstecoren to take charge of the bookselling business while he devoted himself to direction of the press. In 1658, when the University proposed to bring Johannes F. Gronovius to the faculty, Johannes made an additional offer to Gronovius of one hundred gold Philips per year in return for guidance in preparation of a series of classics he proposed to issue. It appears characteristic of Johannes that the engagement with Gronovius was never completed; the contract with Gerstecoren was broken off; and the series of classics never published. Beginning about 1658, it is difficult to determine exactly what was Johannes' intent. In September of that year he petitioned the University curators for permission to enlarge his press building on University land. The august body duly deputized three gentlemen to inspect the site of the proposed enlargement, who, in turn, specified how alterations were to be carried out. In April of the following year Johannes' associate, Gerstecoren, petitioned the curators to be allowed to take over the Elsevier retail store on University land 'upon payment to the rentmaster of the University the yearly rent by which the aforesaid Elsevier had the use of the aforesaid ground,' a request which was laid aside for further consideration and never again appeared in the records.

Between the time Elsevier asked permission to enlarge his press and the time Gerstecoren petitioned to occupy the retail store Johannes began liquidation of his retail book stock. He held the first sale on 10 February, 1659; a second sale followed on 31 May, 1660; and on 12 June he sold to the printer Jan Maire books to the amount of six hundred florins. The sale catalogue of 31 May, 1660, is of interest since it indicates the character of the Elsevier stock. The number and kind of books for sale were as follows:

Theology	212 items	Spanish	5 items
Law	261 items	English	2 items
Medicine	139 items	German	35 items
French	223 items	Netherlands	10 items
Italian	113 items	Miscellaneous	371 items

As for Johannes' printing activities after 1655, they appear largely concerned with work begun before that date, publications issued in his capacity as University printer, or works printed for other booksellers. Production volume was as high as that of his predecessors, but imagination was lacking. At least fifteen per cent of items issued were reprints of works printed by earlier Elseviers, and twenty per cent were produced for other booksellers. After the departure of Daniël, Johannes continued as University printer. As such, his career was uneventful. On one occasion (in August, 1656) the librarian, Thysius, complained to the curators that Elsevier was dilatory in getting out a new edition of *Athenae Batavae*, to which Elsevier replied that plates for the book had long since been finished. The following February Thysius pointed out that as a matter of fact, although he himself had several plates cut for the edition at his own cost, Elsevier had not had a single plate made. The only plates Elsevier possessed were old, well-worn ones from an old edition which, Thysius adds, he had dug out of a corner, and that in spite of Elsevier's protestations six months previous, the book had not yet been printed.

Johannes lived only until June, 1661, and after his death business was carried on by his widow, Eva van Alphen. On 7 November of the same year the curators acceded to the widow's petition asking she be allowed to continue as University printer. They granted her the same conditions accorded her late husband, but stipulated that work begun by him should be completed, especially the new edition of *Athenae Batavae* which had not as yet appeared. Under the widow Elsevier activity of the press decreased greatly. Where her predecessors averaged about twenty books yearly she averaged less than three, and the large majority of these were done for the University or printed for other booksellers. Also, her husband had taken some part in the profitable business of reprinting books issued in France, but in this she took no part. What little of her late husband's retail stock remained she sold, and, as has been noted, she auctioned the book stock at The Hague.

In one respect Johannes' widow strengthened the position of the firm. She proposed to the curators (in November, 1666) that no theses, poems, songs, or other University publications should be printed by anyone other than herself. The request was sustained and the beadle ordered to see to it that only University publications so printed were posted or distributed. Such are the evils of monopoly that in the time of Eva van Alphen there appeared the first of a long series of complaints about the manner in which theses were printed. In November, 1672, the professors complained that both inaugural and ordinary disputations were printed too late, and misprints were not corrected. Although the widow promised to make amends to the best of her ability, five years later (in July, 1677) almost all of the professors again complained that inaugural and other disputations were not appearing at appointed times, to the disadvantage of students and discredit of the University, and it was resolved to admonish the printer she should either employ more apprentices or pass work on to other firms. If there were no improvement in the situation the academic senate resolved to try to have other printers employed.

The widow continued as University printer until May, 1681, when she turned over the office and entire business to her son, Abraham. That gentleman was a person of importance. He was advocate at the Court of Holland at The Hague, doctor of laws from the University of Leyden, and sometime sheriff and councilman for Leyden. In spite of his eminence, his negligence and inefficiency as printer, as will be demonstrated, were appalling. Complaints about workmanship, begun under his mother's regime, multiplied under his. About six weeks after he took office there was a complaint in academic senate by Theodorus Craanen, member of the medical faculty, about the exorbitant price charged a candidate in the medical school for printing his thesis, and the poor paper on which it was printed. The senate resolved to try to get an agreement with the Elseviers on fair prices, but the widow, speaking for the firm, refused to alter the charges, although she was willing to grant a rebate to those who, because of their poverty, would ask her the favor. Her attitude displeased the professorial body, and in the month following (July, 1681) they asked the curators either to lay down a fair price to which the Elseviers would be bound to adhere, or else to cancel the contract with them. But the curators were not to be pushed into impetuous decisions. Four months later (in November) they decided Abraham should keep his office, that he should charge no more than four guilders for a printed signature, that he should charge a reasonable price for paper, and that disputes between printer and students should be judged by the rector and senate on the basis of allowing the printer a reasonable profit. In March of the following year, notwithstanding, Abraham admitted to the academic senate that he had charged the students five guilders per signature instead of four, and he was admonished not to act contrary to the agreement in future. Twelve years later, recurring to an ancient theme,

the academic senate concluded that inasmuch as dissertations were printed on poor paper with worn types,
that corrections of typographic errors were slovenly,
that no proof-readers were employed, that printing
was too long delayed, and that there were cases of
extortion from students, a faculty representative should
have a serious talk with Elsevier. This was done, and
Elsevier promised to mend his ways. He asked that the
matter be not reported to the curators, and this request
was acceded to. It is strange that in the very year his
grievous shortcomings were thus catalogued, the curators
resolved that, after his mother's death, they would pay
Abraham the three hundred guilders which they had
continued to pay her as University printer. It will be
remembered this was exactly the sum they had refused to
pay Bonaventura and his partner, the outstanding
printers in Holland in their time. In October, 1698, the
curators also confirmed to Abraham the monopoly on
theses, songs, poems, and other University pieces granted
originally to his mother, and the beadle was again forbidden to distribute or post publications not printed by
the official printer.

The next year (in November, 1699) Abraham attempted to raise printing prices. He reported to the
curators he had investigated prices paid to other University printers, especially those paid at the University of
Utrecht, and had found the printer there charged five
guilders for printing a signature whereas he was allowed
to charge only four. He declared he could not sell thesis
paper as cheaply as could the man at Utrecht because of
the difference in printing costs, and prayed he be allowed
to charge the same prices as were charged at the neighbor-
ing university. He considered the request especially just

in view of the sad fact that recently his annual stipend had been reduced by one hundred guilders. The rector and senate, in reply to this request, stated that for many years, indeed as long as any of them had sat in the senate, there had been numerous complaints from students arising from the exclusive right to print theses given to Elsevier. There had been long delays, and the printers frequently extorted money from their clients. But the chief complaint concerned high prices charged for paper and printing, causing students to go to Utrecht for graduation to avoid the printer at Leyden. It was true, difficulties about printing prices had been solved by the curators' decision of November, 1681, fixing the maximum charge at four guilders per signature. There remained numerous difficulties about paper prices, the printers charging exorbitant prices despite the curators' decision and the senate's protests. As for Elsevier's contention that five guilders was charged at Utrecht for a signature he printed at Leyden for four, it happened the format of Utrecht theses was such that a gathering there was one-and-a-fourth times as large as a Leyden thesis. In reality, then, prices were equal, except that the Utrecht printer corrected the first proof at his own expense. Moreover, it could not be true, the senate memorial continued, that the printer would suffer if he received only four guilders per signature, since it was easily ascertainable that five hundred copies of a signature filled with Greek and Hebrew could be printed for only three-and-a-half guilders, whereas inaugural dissertations were issued in editions of only two hundred and fifty or three hundred copies. Concerning paper, the professors believed that delivered by Elsevier for eleven *stuivers* a sheet was poorer and browner than that sold at Utrecht for six and eight, and they offered the curators evidence to prove the point. Rector and senate felt the data in the printer's petition were at variance with the truth, yet they were inclined to grant Elsevier the Utrecht price of five guilders per signature, provided all other conditions in force at Utrecht regarding proof-readers, format, and paper were adhered to. The verbal bludgeoning evidently had some slight effect, for in July, 1700, Elsevier solemnly promised he would furnish theses in the same format, on the same quality paper as those printed at Utrecht, and for the same price, a promise he soon proceeded to break. In July, 1703, for example, he admitted he had been using poor paper and promised in future to use the quality of paper his contract called for; he asked to be allowed to increase the charge for paper since the price had gone up. At the same time he explained he did not use proof-readers because many students did not wish to have them. Five years later it is again wearily noted in the academic senate records that the printer used the poorest kind of paper, substituting without notice a poor grade for the grade agreed upon, that he extorted exorbitant prices for it, and that typographic errors remained uncorrected. His shortcomings were laid before the curators, who again admonished him to mend his ways, suggesting if he did not they would take less agreeable measures. In 1711 the senate was also complaining about the chickens and dogs around the Elsevier establishment which created a tremendous noise and a great deal of dirt, and the beadle was instructed to notify Elsevier to remove the offending fauna from the University yard.

Bereft alike of proofreaders, chickens and dogs, the press continued on its way to perdition. A German traveler, Dr Lämmermann, visiting Leyden in 1710 wrote that, 'The Elsevier press, which formerly was so justly famous, has now greatly declined, and appears to fall lower daily because the proprietor, Abraham Elsevier, is a sheriff or alderman of the city while he neglects the press, and also he is not sufficiently learned. At the least, one can say truthfully that nowhere in Europe is printing done in a more vicious manner than here. Journeymen act as though they are the masters, and make corrections only when they are good and ready. For the most part Elsevier prints theses, of which there are an unbelievable number defended here. If students were not forced to have their theses printed here, and if Elsevier were not an alderman of the city, he would certainly have to eat small crumbs. The price of the printed sheet is five guilders; black paper costs five-and-a-half *stuivers*, ordinary paper twelve *stuivers*, and good paper one guilder two *stuivers*, so the cost of a small thesis may easily be from sixty to seventy guilders. The building is in the form of a square with two passages. There are many type cases, but only four presses, and of these only one, or at most two, is in daily use.'

Where Elseviers had at times published on the average twenty books per year, and even Abraham's mother had averaged three, he did not average more than one. He died on 30 July, 1712. With a certain unseemly haste, on the eighth of August a representative of the academic senate appeared before the curators and reminded them of the inconveniences, injuries and uninspired printing which had been the lot of the University under the mal-administration of the late lamented Elsevier. He had used poor paper and bad types and had charged too much. He had not corrected proofs and many times inaugural and other theses had not appeared on time. Results of these conditions were that the luster of the University was dimmed, that students were forced to have theses reprinted, and many times went to Utrecht or elsewhere to graduate. In spite of good resolutions, regulations, penalties earlier imposed and promises made, no redress for the grievances had been found. The representative asked, on behalf of the faculty, that printing be handled as it had been before the Elseviers obtained a monopoly; specifically, that the University printer be paid only for work the curators and burgomasters asked him to print, and that students be allowed to have theses printed, or at least buy paper for them, where they pleased and where they were best served. But if it were decided to appoint a printer under the same conditions enjoyed by Abraham, then the faculty asked it be a man who well understood both printing and bookselling, that all rules designed to insure good typography formerly promulgated be renewed or amplified and also that penalties be inflicted upon the University printer if he did not fulfill his obligations. As a matter of fact, the prime reason for engaging a University printer soon vanished. Abraham's widow decided to sell the oriental press, and as the University could not afford to buy it, the press passed out of academic control. Jacob Poereep, the beadle, was appointed printer in October, 1712, and thereafter students were allowed to have theses printed where they desired.

As one reads the shabby account of the last Leyden Elsevier one wonders why the University suffered so long the disservice of an ignorant and negligent man. In the Holland of the period members of the ruling, or regent, class, too often considered public offices existed for their benefit, that salaries were to be enjoyed, that there were no obligations. This may have been Elsevier's attitude,

95

for he was an office holder and well connected, being a member of the city council and, in 1710, sheriff of the city. His grandfather, Daniël van Alphen, was councilor and burgomaster of the city, and, it will be remembered, burgomasters joined with the curators in governing the University. Also, in the memoranda of Elsevier which have survived, there is a certain superficial plausibility. This may be indicative of his character; his contemporaries probably were never quite certain of his insincerity. Certainly there had been great changes in the relations of Elseviers with the University. Some hundred and twenty-five years earlier the University had given Louis an opportunity to exist. He had eagerly and cheerfully bound and procured books for the academy, and had run its errands over Europe. In return the University increased its favors and honored him and his descendants with office. The relationship ended with his great-great-grandson, the successful lawyer, the municipal politician, milking students and University by furnishing shoddy work at shameful prices.

Johannes and Eva Elsevier had two sons: the elder, who went away to sea and became vice-admiral of Holland and West Friesland, and the younger, the gentleman just discussed. Possibly if Leyden and the University had continued to expand and prosper, or if the firm had grasped new opportunities developing in the commerce of books, the able admiral would have been encouraged to stay home and save his house from the sad ending which has been narrated. But, fortunately for the Elseviers, their fame has not rested entirely on the work of the Leyden firm. In the last half of the seventeenth century members of the family established at Amsterdam won wider respect and renown than the Leyden house ever possessed, and the Amsterdam establishment will next be considered.

96

6

The Amsterdam House
Louis and Daniël Elsevier

THE Amsterdam branch of the Elsevier house was established in 1638 by Louis Elsevier, son of Joost, who before removing to Amsterdam had been employed by his relatives at Leyden. He conducted the business alone until 1655, when he was joined by his cousin Daniël, and from that date, or soon after, the Amsterdam house was the chief Elsevier establishment. As the reader will remember, this was not the only branch establishment; there had been ventures at Utrecht and Copenhagen. The Amsterdam offshoot was the biggest and most successful, partly because Amsterdam was thriving and prosperous, one of the most important commercial centers of Europe. Back in 1585 the Spanish had recaptured Antwerp from rebellious Netherlanders. The Dutch, who controlled the mouth of the Scheldt, promptly closed it to shipping, and strangled the commercial life of Antwerp. Amsterdam largely inherited the commerce. The war with Spain brought other advantages. As subjects of Spain the Dutch were barred from oversea markets of the metropolis, but being in open rebellion, they could exploit and raid the Spanish colonial empire. The accelerated expansion of trade after the revolt is evident in the convoy and license money (port charges) collected by the admiralty of Amsterdam. In 1589, soon

97

after the closing of the Scheldt, the total collected was about two hundred and fifty thousand guilders. In 1620 the amount collected was approximately three hundred and ten per cent of that sum. By 1638 (the year Louis Elsevier established himself at Amsterdam) the revenue was about four hundred and twenty-three per cent of what it had been in 1589. During the wars of the latter half of the century shipping suffered greatly, but by the century's end the revenue from convoy and license money was, in round figures, eight hundred and five per cent of the 1589 total. The city enjoyed a major share of Netherlands shipping, and although comprehensive statistics on shipping are complicated, an indication of Amsterdam's share is given by the following group of figures: in the period from 25 June to 16 November, 1645 (less than five months), seven hundred and thirty-five specifically named ships passed in through the Sound, the narrow seas between the Baltic and the Cattegat. There are data on six hundred and ninety-four of these, six hundred and forty-five of which had sailed from Dutch ports, and of the latter number, three hundred and fifty-nine, or more than half, had sailed from Amsterdam. In the same period, of seven hundred and ninety-three expressly named ships sailing from Baltic ports, seven hundred and two were bound for Dutch coast cities, and five hundred and ninety, or more than two-thirds, were bound for Amsterdam. The great trading companies had their headquarters here. When the East India Company was organized in 1602 a capital of six and one-half million guilders was raised, more than six times, incidentally, the amount collected to launch the British East India Company. The Company was largely an Amsterdam venture. By the charter provisions, Amsterdam participants

98

held half the shares; the Amsterdam chamber named eight members of the seventeen constituting the 'Collegium,' the Company's governing body. Probably about half the Netherlands East India trade was in the hands of Amsterdam men. They participated also in the West India Company, and enjoyed a large share of Dutch trade to south Europe, the Levant, the Baltic, and Scandinavian countries.

The city was not wholly dependent on commerce. It also played a part in Holland's flourishing industries; the most important of these was the fishery, but there were others. Thus, although Leyden was a great cloth-making center, textiles were manufactured in Amsterdam too, and in addition there was extensive trading there in cloth and wool. In 1608–9 excise collected on woolen cloth at Amsterdam was sixty-nine thousand guilders, whereas at Leyden in the same period, the amount collected was seven thousand guilders. The great growth of the Leyden industry occurred after these years, but the statistic is helpful in understanding the scope of Amsterdam activities. In addition to competing with Leyden in woolen fabrics, the city competed with Haarlem in linens, and in dyeing and weaving silk it was pre-eminent. An eighteenth-century merchant, looking back on the good old days, avowed that 'I believe it to be a fact that formerly the fabrication of silk and silk cloth alone maintained in our land more men in work and prosperity and thus yielded more profit than is now yielded by the whole East India Company.' The manufacture of silk led to the manufacture of satins, and well into the eighteenth century Amsterdam held the leadership in this textile. The city had been an important silk market in the latter half of the preceding century. The actual manufacture of silk had been partly

99

the result of chance. In February, 1603, Holland's famous admiral, Jacob van Heemskerk, captured the Portuguese carack, *Santa Catharina*, in the Straits of Malacca, and a few months later Admiral Wybrandt van Warwijck captured another rich ship before Macao. The *Santa Catharina* alone had on board twelve hundred bales of silk, worth two and a quarter million guilders. As a consequence (in August, 1604), a great auction of Chinese silk was held in Amsterdam. Silk merchants streamed to the city from all over Europe. The burgomasters were anxious that the silk be worked up in Amsterdam itself, and in September, 1604, they gave to one Emanual Rodrigos, Portuguese, for four or five years rent free, a house on the Boerenverdriet which was lengthened to accommodate two mills for the working of Chinese silk, with the proviso that Rodrigos would teach others the trade. A few months later the municipality bought up, for the benefit of the new industry, great quantities of raw silk, the city fathers considering that not only would trade and prosperity be increased by the new industry, but also that the East India Company trade would be greatly advanced, and consequently large numbers of humble and poor people enabled to earn a livelihood.

In addition to excelling in silk industries Amsterdam stood first in sugar refining. One writer believed that, before 1660, there were approximately as many refiners in the city as there were in the rest of Christendom. At the end of the century a memorial of sugar refiners stated that their industry had become one of the most considerable and heavily capitalized in the city, that in flourishing times more than a hundred large merchantmen were employed to bring in raw sugar, and that weighage money paid by refiners in such times was about one-fifth of all weighage paid in a year to the collector of excise. In addition to what has been mentioned, there was also a tobacco industry, considerable brewing, large scale trading in grain and timber, and, most colorful of all, a brisk trade in tulip bulbs.

The growth of commerce and industry demanded a strong bank. The Amsterdam Exchange Bank was founded by the municipality in 1609. In that first year, seven hundred and thirty-one accounts were opened. The number of accounts increased one hundred per cent by 1641, and more than two hundred per cent by the end of the century. In the first year after the Bank's founding there were deposited, in round figures, nine hundred and twenty-five thousand guilders. By 1650 the deposits had grown to nearly twelve million. Banking, like other activities, suffered much in the war years of the second half of the century, but nevertheless by 1699 deposits totaled roughly sixteen million, seven hundred and fifty thousand guilders. Expansion of banking and industry was accompanied by remarkable population increase. The Venetian ambassador estimated, and obviously underestimated, that in 1610 the municipal population stood at fifty thousand. In 1622 it was about one hundred thousand; in 1630, about one hundred and fifteen thousand. After that date, growth was accelerated. An estimate of 1632 gave the figure one hundred and twenty-five thousand; in 1642 it was about one hundred and forty-five thousand; in 1652, one hundred and seventy thousand; 1662, two hundred thousand. Thereafter there is a dearth of statistics, but it is probable the population remained not far from the latter figure for the remainder of the century. The first official census in 1795 placed the population at about two hundred and twenty-one thousand. A concomitant to population growth was an increasing city area, many of Amsterdam's finest streets and canals being constructed in this century.

Industrial and commercial power brought in its wake cultural and intellectual development. As in the history of our American cities, this was at first crude and imitative, but eventually deep, strong, and in some phases, but not all, original. The theatre had a great vogue; in Amsterdam it fell under the spell of French classicism. The plays of Corneille and his imitators were popular, and Molière also was much admired. Painting was an industry in which practitioners were highly specialized. Rich burghers had portraits of themselves and families, and pictures of their houses and jewels. Even the sight of their rich foods was preserved, arousing the envy and whetting the appetite of future generations. Out of the plethora of painting came some glories of our civilization. Rembrandt lived the greater part of his life in Amsterdam, finding there the vitality and variety his broad genius demanded. His presence brought Nicolaes Maes, Ferdinand Bol, Carel Fabritius, and many another painter to the city. In the town lived the landscape painters Hercules Seghers and Jacob van Ruisdael, and the animal painter Adriaen van der Velde. Gabriël Metsu and Pieter de Hooch were also citizens. The founding of the University of Amsterdam in 1632 and the presence of many flourishing literary societies stimulated intellectual pursuits and a demand for books.

As in Leyden, the book trade in Amsterdam experienced amazing growth in the era. In the first quarter of the seventeenth century ninety-six firms operated for longer or shorter periods; in the second quarter there were one hundred and fifty-four firms; in the third, one hundred and ninety; and in the last quarter, two hundred and seventy-three. Of Dutch cities, Leyden was second to Amsterdam in number of booksellers, and not a good second. In the last quarter of the century the number of dealers operating at Amsterdam was three times the number at Leyden. Further indication of growth in the book trade is afforded by statistics on booksellers visiting the Frankfurt book fair, where Amsterdam men dominated a powerful Dutch delegation. The important position the Dutch occupied is indicated by the fact that in 1669 they threatened the Frankfurt council that if they were not freed from harassing regulations they would boycott the fair. In the first decade of the century four Amsterdam dealers made seventeen journeys to Frankfurt. The numbers increased more or less steadily until the 1660s when thirty-nine dealers made one hundred and twenty-nine visits to the fair. The numbers dwindled following the sixties, not because Amsterdam trade fell off, but chiefly because the fair gradually lost importance. In the last decade of the century fourteen dealers made twenty-five visits. Evidently, then, when Louis Elsevier located there, Amsterdam was a promising place for the book business, and he was himself prepared to make the venture successful, having been reared in the milieu of bookmen. His father, Joost, had sold books for a time at Utrecht, and after finishing his studies in philosophy at the University of Leyden, Louis had entered the Elsevier Leyden firm, Bonaventura being his uncle and Abraham his cousin. His work on this occasion may be described by the statement that he was traveling salesman, and his territory western Europe. Students of Elsevier history have gathered fragments of evidence on his travels. In

May, 1632, he was in Denmark, and returned there two years later. He was in Italy in 1636, and saw there his friend Lucas Holstenius, librarian to Cardinal Barberini. The next year he was again in Denmark. In the same year (1637) he took up citizenship in Amsterdam, and the year following severed his connection with the Leyden house and established a book business there. It was perhaps apparent to him, since both partners, Bonaventura and Abraham, had sons destined for the book trade, his future with the Leyden house was not promising. Reflection on the character of Louis' friends makes apparent another reason for striking out for himself. A great many whom he found congenial were tainted with heresy; whereas his employers, Bonaventura and Abraham, maintained unsullied orthodoxy. Among Louis' friends was Gerardus Vossius who held various offices at Leyden University and had, like many others, experienced ill-will and difficulties in 1619 because of Remonstrant sympathies. Later he joined the faculty at Amsterdam. Meursius, another friend, had also been associated with the Remonstrants. He became a professor at Sorø, finding the atmosphere at the Danish university more congenial than orthodox Leyden. Hugo Grotius had, of course, been condemned by the Contra-Remonstrants. Johannes Corvinus had been a pastor at Leyden, a leader in the Remonstrant movement, and consequently lost his place in 1619. Etienne Courcelles, a French Huguenot pastor, also unable to stomach the strict doctrine of predestination, had settled at Amsterdam. Since these gentlemen were Louis' friends or acquaintances, it is possible he permitted himself a latitude in belief not countenanced by his relatives. He may have been spoiled by travel: to have lived in France and Italy, to have known many Catholics and liked them, made it difficult to remain a strict Calvinist. At Amsterdam he took a place on the Damrak, a canal whose borders were favored by booksellers, Joan Blaeu, Jan Janszoon, Waesberghe, and many others being in the neighborhood.

The break with the Leyden firm was amicable. Leyden publications were sold at Louis' Amsterdam shop, and when he could issue books himself the first ventures were printed by Bonaventura and Abraham. Louis' publication list is an interesting one. His business was new, and he did not print and reprint well-tried favorites. Not being associated with a university he felt no compulsion to print classics, theology, and scholarly paraphernalia. The number of books published increased more or less steadily. In each of the years 1649 and 1650 he issued twenty-three books, more than the total number issued in these years by his distinguished relatives at Leyden. He published, among other interesting titles, *Elementa philosophica de cive* of Thomas Hobbes (1647); Francis Bacon's *Scripta in naturali et universali philosophia* (1653) and *Sylva sylvarum* (1648); Gassendi's *Exercitationes paradoxicae adversus Aristoteleos* (1649); and John Milton's *Defense of the English people* (1651). He also issued the original edition of Pieter C. Hooft's *History of the Netherlands from the time of the handing over the Dominion by Charles V to King Philip his son*, one of the greatest works of Dutch prose. Most noteworthy were publications centering around Descartes. He issued at least seven different titles by Descartes, a number of them in more than one edition. He printed also the efforts of the great scientist's ardent, if sometimes ill informed, partisans. Clauberg, Hogelande, Tobias Andreae, Wittichius were all issued by him. Johannes Clauberg's defense of Cartesianism against attacks leveled upon it by

Cyriacus Lentulus, professor at Herborn, and Revius, a Leyden theologian, appeared in 1652. The defense of Descartes by Tobias Andreae against criticism by Henri Regius, professor of medicine at Utrecht, was issued in 1653. In the same year appeared a rational discussion of some of the points of difference between Cartesianism and its opponents by a pillar of Cartesianism, Christophoro Wittichius, then a professor at Duisburg. Earlier, in 1646, Louis published the *Cogitations* of Cornelis Hogelande which purported to be an interpretation of Cartesian principles, but of which it was said there was nothing in it of Descartes except the dedication, Descartes himself mildly remarking of Hogelande, 'I do not even believe that he has read my works thoroughly.'

At Leyden Louis had inclined to Arminianism when it would have been opportune to be a Gomarist. One is inclined to think he published the authors he did, scientists and liberal theologians, because he had a predilection for them, rather than because he merely found it profitable; in any event, his business prospered. In 1640 he bought a small press and no longer relied completely on others for printing. He took his cousin Daniël into the firm in 1655, and from that date Amsterdam was the principal Elsevier establishment. In 1664 Louis retired and turned over the direction of affairs to Daniël. After retirement he spent much time at his country place, to which he was much attached, and upon which he spent large sums. Without wife or children himself, he was sheet anchor, guide and mentor for multitudinous Elsevier relatives. He developed the avocation early in life. When twenty-one, he witnessed the agreement by which cousin Isaac sold his printing equipment to Bonaventura and Abraham. In the same year he witnessed a contract between these partners and

Jacob Elsevier for the sale of books at The Hague. His mother's will of April, 1642, requested he be guardian for his sister's four young children; when his brother Pieter died he became guardian for Pieter's three children; and when his uncle Bonaventura died he assumed a third guardianship, taking responsibility for his uncle's minor children. Louis died in 1670. Characteristically his will provided his sister, Maria, should receive a third of his estate and that the remaining two-thirds should be divided between children and grandchildren of his sister Barbara, the children of his brother Pieter, and his cousin Daniël. Minor details of his will convey the impression of a kindly, sentimental man, as when he provided that a silver and gilt cup which had come from Nuremburg (together with a thousand guilders) should be given to his godchild, Louis Elsevier, and an annuity of four hundred guilders be paid his old servant, Maartgen Daniels, together with the gift of a bed, bed clothes, household goods and some of the poorest pictures, at the discretion of the executors. To the poor of 's-Graveland where he had his country place he left six hundred guilders, the interest from which was to buy them clothing or fulfil their other needs. His death had little effect on the business since its direction had been in the hands of Daniël since 1664, six years before his death. Daniël, son of Bonaventura, had succeeded to his father's share of the Leyden business and had carried on in partnership with his nephew Johannes. He left Leyden and joined Louis at Amsterdam three months after his marriage in 1655 to Anna Beerninck, one of Louis' wards. Doubtless this was a change for the better. His partner Johannes at Leyden showed no particular promise; Amsterdam was a wider field of endeavor, and his cousin Louis, then past fifty, had a prosperous business.

At Leyden Daniël had acted as traveling agent for the firm. Upon joining the Amsterdam house he assumed the same duties, visiting Germany and France, and later making several journeys to England. He enlarged the bookselling branch, amassing large stocks of new and antiquarian books, and carried forward publishing with energy. He had a capacity for attracting able men to his employ. Simon Moynet, corrector of the press at Leyden, left that city and joined Daniël at Amsterdam as proofreader. About 1667 Jacob de Zetter, who had been a modest bookseller and publisher in Amsterdam, joined his *ménage* and remained with the firm until its dissolution. About two years later (in 1669) he employed Henri Wetstein, son of a professor at Basle, who worked with him seven years and later founded the famous publishing house which endured for nearly eight decades.

Daniël was able to give impetus to the publication program, since he inherited rights to a large number of Leyden publications. In his first five years with the Amsterdam firm more than twenty per cent of the publications had been issued previously at Leyden. He also decreased the number of books in Latin. When Louis worked alone about eighty-one per cent of the books were in Latin; while Louis and Daniël were both active about seventy-three per cent of items printed or published by them were in that language, whereas from Louis' retirement until the death of Daniël only about fifty-two per cent of the books were in classic languages; the remainder, with the exception of a few in Italian, were in French, a language increasingly used by the learned. Pierre Bayle wrote (in 1685) concerning the Netherlands that, 'The French language is so well known in this country that more French books are sold here than all others. There is hardly a man of letters who does not understand French although they do not know how to speak it. Latin is not so widely known . . . ' The firm's volume of printing and publishing also increased slightly. Louis, before Daniël's coming, averaged about thirteen books per year. While the men were in partnership they averaged about seventeen per annum, and after Louis retired Daniël issued an average of fifteen books annually. The latter record is remarkable since during the period Holland was cursed with disastrous war.

As had Louis before him, Daniël printed works by Erasmus and Bacon, and also continued to issue books by Descartes and about Cartesianism. As a result, he was looked to as a source of information on Descartes and his followers. Thus Nicolas-Joseph Poisson, Oratorian father and enthusiastic Cartesian, sought information on Descartes' life in Holland. Daniël replied, 'It will be very difficult, Sir, to give you any account of Descartes' life during his stay in this country, or at least anything worthy to report of so great a man. I have spoken to people who consider him a demi-god; they say to me that Monsieur Descartes himself described the principle by which he lived in his *Discourse on Method,* that all that one knows of him here is only a confused memory, not worthy of that author. When I go to Leyden I shall speak of him to one of his old friends and let you know what he has to say.' Antoinette de Bourignon, a curious female theologian, also wrote Daniël asking him to arrange an interview for her with Heydanus, a well-known Cartesian.

Aside from a leaning toward Cartesianism, Daniël's publishing exhibited a predilection for Jansenist works. He issued (1657) the Provincials of Pascal, disguising the fact with the imprint, 'At Cologne, at the shop of Pierre de la Vallée,' and he also brought out Nicolle's Latin translation of the Provincials. An *Explanation of the facts and sense of Jansenius* with the imprint 'At Cologne,' appeared in 1660. In 1662 he published, without placing his name in the imprint, *Journal de Mr de Saint Amour*, which was ordered burned by the hangman since several ecclesiastical gentlemen found it contained the five propositions of Jansen. He printed also the *Constitutions of Port Royal*, and the *Mons New Testament* for Gaspard Migeot, a bookseller at Mons.

A striking characteristic of Daniel Elsevier's list is the large number of books by Molière. Louis and Daniël, or Daniël alone, published twenty-four separate plays by this author, several of them in more than one edition, and two editions of Molière's works. All classes in Holland enjoyed the playwright. In addition to numerous French editions, seventeen of his plays appeared in Dutch during the century, some in more than one translation. The types of books not printed by Daniël are worth noting. Holland enjoyed more freedom of the press than any country in Europe. As a consequence Dutch publishers and booksellers did a thriving business in books it was unwise to handle in other lands: attacks on English Puritans or Royalists, or exposés of French court scandals, for example. Occasionally one Dutch authority or another condemned books as being obscene or irreligious, or because they were likely to offend foreign governments. It is to the Elseviers' credit that none of their publications was condemned as salacious, or offensive to Holland's neighbors, and only two were condemned on religious grounds. These could hardly be termed scandalous. Descartes' letter in reply to his arch-enemy, Voetius, the great professor of theology at Utrecht, first printed by Louis

before Daniël joined the firm and reprinted many times
later, was forbidden by Utrecht municipal authorities.
The second of the condemned books, Isaac La Peyrère's
Pre-Adamites, was published by Louis and Daniël in 1655.
This work, which postulated a race of men existing before
Adam, was ordered burned by the public hangman, the
States General judging it 'directly contrary to God's Holy
Word, and the true reformed Christian religion.'

Through publishing and bookselling Daniël knew men
in all stations and nations. The Duke of Montausier wrote
requesting he print an edition of Festus. Philippus
Munckerus, who held the office of rector at Deventer,
Haarlem and Arnhem, wanted published his treatise *De
Intercalatione variarum gentium et praesertim Romanorum*; and
Graevius submitted for publication a collection of
unpublished letters of Morin, Aléandre, Pierre de la Vallé,
Peiresc, Chapelain, and Buxtorf. Daniël also corresponded
with Émeric Bigot, a Norman bibliophile widely known
among men of letters. He was a firm friend of Johann
Benedikt Carpzov, Leyden graduate and classical scholar,
and an acquaintance, at least, of the elegant Constantijn
Huygens. His friend, Nicolas Thoynard, bibliophile and
author, had ideas for improving the art of printing. He
advocated casting two letter combinations, printing two
formes simultaneously, precisely how is not clear, and
forming stereotype plates. Daniël reported to Thoynard
objections of his type-founder to the schemes, and added
his own criticism on printing two formes simultaneously,
saying the idea was useless, and a folly impossible of
realization. Men of letters valued his friendship. Ezechiel
Spanheim, scholar, writer, and resident for the Electoral
Palatinate and Brandenburg at London, recommended
Daniël as a man with a 'name and a merit known to all

those who love letters and the sciences.' Louis Gorin de
Saint Amour, in a preface to a French grammar issued in
1678, wrote that, ' ... Mr Daniël Elsevier of Amsterdam, a
man celebrated for his abilities and for the beautiful
volumes which he publishes, will not be grieved if it is
made known that it is to him the public is indebted for
this grammar,' and he goes on to say it had been his good
fortune to be a traveling companion of Mr Elsevier in a
journey from Frankfurt to Amsterdam, and that Mr
Elsevier remarked upon the need for a good French
grammar. Saint Amour, accordingly, upon his return to
France undertook to have one written, and when difficulties appeared Mr Elsevier encouraged him to persevere.

Daniël Elsevier's great friend among scholars was
Nicolaas Heinsius. In a manner Nicolaas was to him what
Daniël Heinsius had been to Leyden Elseviers, although
Daniël Elsevier stood in less need of scholarly guidance
than had his forefathers. Throughout a diplomat's busy
life Nicolaas Heinsius continued to edit Latin poets and
to write poetry. Being a poet, he excelled in conjectural
emendation, earning the soubriquet, 'Preserver of Latin
Poets.' The Elseviers published many of his editions, and
Heinsius was never out of touch with affairs at the Amsterdam press. The friendship of the two men endured
thirty-five years. Letters of Elsevier to his friend for part
of the period (May 1675-July 1679) are extant. In them,
the writer mentions books he and his contemporaries are
publishing and discusses problems connected with them.
He reports the receipt or non-receipt of messages and
packages, and frequently the letters end with the latest
war news and peace rumors. The correspondents were
much preoccupied with the latter subject. Heinsius was
preparing for Elsevier an edition of Virgil intended to be

dedicated to Louis XIV, and Holland's war with France made the dedication awkward. The difficulty was solved by issuing a trade edition without dedication while war was in progress, and a large paper edition, with dedication, after war had ceased. To Elsevier's chagrin, the date of the earlier edition remained on the engraved title-page of the later edition. The letters of Elsevier are not remarkable, but they are evidence of enduring friendship between a great publisher and a fine scholar.

In addition to extensive acquaintance with authors, Daniël formed widespread connections with booksellers. Surviving documents show that in 1680 he sent four bales of books to Nantes by the skipper Jonge Foppe, one bale for Henry de Graef, a bookseller of the city, one to be forwarded to Tours, and one each to be sent to the towns of Vannes and Saumur. Incidentally, the bales were never delivered, being confiscated by the King's attorney of the high court of Nantes, while Foppe's ship lay in the river, because the bales contained La Peyrère's *Pre-Adamites*, but the transaction indicates Elsevier had connections with provincial as well as Parisian booksellers. Elsewhere is recorded an engagement Elsevier entered into with a Parisian, Thomas Joly, merchant bookseller at the palais in the parish of Saint Bartholomew, whom he speaks of as being his old friend. Joly having fallen on evil days, Daniël advanced him enough merchandise to re-establish himself and alleviate the distress of himself and family. There is ample evidence he transacted business in Germany also, but more interesting for English readers are the journeys he made to England.

Surviving evidence of his activity in that country is extensive. Possibly it began in 1669 when he assisted Sir William Temple, the British ambassador, and agents of

113

the French government in suppressing scandalous books about the French court. An account of the affair is given elsewhere in this chapter, but an important by-product of it was that it placed Temple under some obligation to Elsevier. Six years later, when Elsevier badly needed English friends, Temple wrote (20 February, 1675) to Sir Joseph Williamson, the Secretary of State, as follows:

Sr. – I could not refuse the bearer a small recommendation which he desireth upon his going into England, nor addresse it as I thought better than to yourselfe whom I know to be a lover of learning & a favourer of those of his profession.His name is Elzevir & he is son of that Elzevir of Leyden, whose print hath run through the world with so much approbation. Himselfe is both a printer & seller of books at Amsterdam & in very good credit there. Some small businesses with his correspondents in London of the same profession draws him now over, but chiefly a desire of seeing England, where he desired some protection in case he should happen to stand in need of it. I thought he might the better deserve it for having shew'd great readinesse & taken some paines as well as been at some losse in executing what His Maty. by me desired during my last Embassage here about the suppressing certain scandalous pamphlets wherein the honour of the Royall family was something interested. When I have said this much I shall need give you no further trouble upon this occasion & will end this with the assurance of my being

Yr most faithfull
humble servant

WM TEMPLE

In favour of
  Mons. Elzevir.

The reason Elsevier needed some protection, and why he went to England, was described in a long letter he wrote (probably in March, 1675) to Williamson. He related that in 1640 Hugo Grotius had given Jan Maire, printer at Leyden, publication rights to his *De Veritate Religionis Christianae*. Some twenty years before writing to Williamson Elsevier had purchased the manuscript from Maire and republished it. The work was later pirated by William Webb, bookseller at Oxford, and after Webb's death his widow sought to sell the rights to this book, and several others by Grotius, to London booksellers. 'But,' says Elsevier, 'since the booksellers saw they would not be able to prevent my impression being sold there, they were not interested in purchasing it.' The widow Webb then approached the Oxford Press authorities who eventually purchased the rights to *De Veritate Religionis Christianae* 'for the low price of about five pounds sterling,' Elsevier was told. 'Last year,' he continued, 'in the month of March, one of the chief booksellers of London wrote me that the Oxford Press had the intention of printing the book. He advised me to send a large number of copies to London to forestall the move, and offered to serve me in the matter. Since I had only three hundred copies on hand, I reprinted two thousand more, all of which I sold to John Dunmore, merchant bookseller in that city, and sent them to him about six months ago.' It then happened, Elsevier relates, that the bookseller who had written him originally was angered to find the copies had been sent to Dunmore and some to Oxford booksellers, and wrote the authorities at the Oxford Press to say there were two thousand copies of Grotius at the custom-house which they had the right to impound. The Oxford Press people acted upon his advice, 'and,' laments Elsevier, 'the books are still in the custom-house.' He then says that every publisher in Europe respects the literary property of his colleagues, it being accounted among them a species of larceny for any one to pirate the works of a competitor.

He cites the example of a German printer who pirated his edition of Quintus Curtius, obtained a privilege to publish it from the Emperor and then sought to prevent Elsevier from selling his copies in Germany. Elsevier carried his case, he says, to the Emperor, with the result that the pirate was forced to pay a fine and Elsevier was allowed to sell his books as before. In this judgment, continues Elsevier, the Emperor's council considered that to decide otherwise was to encourage the inclination and maliciousness of those who, not having the intelligence or skill to invent something themselves, wished to profit by the skill and labor of others. It would be a crowning injustice, the council thought, not to punish those who, not content to have robbed their neighbors, wished moreover to cut their throats. Elsevier's implication is that the Emperor's council handled the case as such affairs ought to be handled. In addition to writing Williamson, Daniël went to Oxford to remonstrate with Dr John Fell about the matter, for on 14 March, 1675, Fell wrote to Williamson to say that, 'I hope I have concluded Mr Elsevirs affair concerning Grotius to his satisfaction; at his return to London he will wait upon you for your Order for the dismission of those Copies which he imported ... ' Accordingly, ten days later the books were released from customs, and four days following Secretary Williamson dismissed the whole matter upon 'an Information which hath been exhibited in Our Court of Exchequer by Our Trusty and Welbeloved John Fell and Thomas Yates, D^{rs} in Div^{ty}.'

The following year Elsevier was involved in an affair *vis-à-vis* his Britannic Majesty's government in which government was not so entirely convinced of his blameless character. At one time (in 1675) Elsevier intended to print Milton's Latin state letters, having arranged to do so with a poor English scholar, Daniel Skinner. But the redoubtable Secretary of State, Williamson, was an anti-Milton man and the project languished until in 1676, as Skinner put it, there crept into the world a little imperfect book of Milton's Latin letters, and Skinner approached Williamson with the request that since one version of the letters was now in print, he be allowed to print his edition. At this stage, two momentous events intervened. First, Skinner, who had been dogged by ill fortune (he was, for example, unable to repay ten pounds borrowed from Samuel Pepys), had an opportunity to procure a post in the British delegation to the peace congress at Nijmegen; and second, about the same time Williamson got wind of another edition of Milton's letters being published, as he thought, at Leyden. Williamson immediately wrote the secretary of the British embassy at The Hague saying that 'His Matie is informed of a pernicious Booke, of that late Villain Milton's, now about to be printed at Leyden, I am commanded to signify to you, that you immediately apply yr selfe, to find out by the best means you may, if there be any such, who is the printer, and by what order he is sett on worke.' Skinner, eager to earn the approbation of Williamson, a powerful man in matters of appointments to embassies, set off post haste to Amsterdam to stop the printing if Elsevier had it in hand. He was overjoyed to find the printing had not even begun, and Elsevier wrote Williamson, who, he avowed, had treated him well when he was in London, to reassure him the letters were not printed, and would not be printed. As for the rumor, Elsevier added, that he planned to print all of Milton's works, 'I protest to you that I have never had a thought about it, and I should have a horror of printing the treatises which he wrote in defense of such a wicked and abominable cause. Moreover, it would hardly be fitting to the son of he who first printed the *Defensio Regia* of Salmasius, and who would have given his life if he had been able to save the late king of glorious memory, to print a book so detested by all honest men.' Later Elsevier wrote Skinner's father to reassure him he had returned the Milton manuscripts to his son, and added that for his part, for a number of reasons, he would not print the thing if he were given a thousand pounds. A book dealer depending on foreign markets could not be embroiled with such a man as Williamson. Two editions of the letters in question did, in fact, appear in 1676; they were both printed by Fricx, and not by Elsevier. As for Skinner, his connection with the villain Milton effectively spoiled his chance for a job in the embassy; and the moral of course, is that young men desiring government jobs should carefully avoid dangerous revolutionaries, like John Milton.

It is helpful sometimes to distinguish between Dutch publishers who took advantage of the freedom of Holland to print scandalous and libelous literature, for which there has always been a demand, and those who, for the sake of international trade, sought, as Elsevier did in the Skinner case, to avoid giving offense to foreign governments. The attitude of the latter group reflected the official government viewpoint. Dutch historians have felt, in fact, that in the seventeenth century government was too fearful of giving offense to Holland's neighbors, too much concerned for peace at any price, too apprehensive of what wars might do to international trade on which the country largely depended. To this attitude, more or less common to solid citizens, may be ascribed an action for which Daniël has been criticized. The incident is described by Elsevier in a document entitled *Memoir of Daniel Elsevier, of what has been done and of what ought to be done to prevent the sale of books injurious to persons of quality and contrary to good manners*, a document which, unfortunately for the writer's status as patriot, was discovered in the Archives de la Bastille. Elsevier relates that in 1667 two books derogatory to Frenchmen of quality appeared in Amsterdam. When they were first published he approached a burgomaster and protested that if something were not done about such books, there would be more of them. As a result the burgomasters summoned certain booksellers, whom Elsevier designated, and commanded them to bring all copies of the two books in question to the Town Hall where they were burned. The following year, Elsevier continues, Monsieur Joly, secretary to the French ambassador to England, being in Amsterdam, heard about the publication of a *History of Madame*, and was anxious to suppress it. He sought out the publishers and bought up the whole edition of fifteen hundred copies. These were baled and Joly requested Elsevier to hold the bales subject to his instructions. Subsequently he indicated Sir William Temple, the British ambassador, would handle the matter, and Temple sent his secretary to ask Elsevier to burn the books, which was done 'without anyone's being present except ourselves,' says Elsevier, 'and not a single leaf escaped us.' It was this service, incidentally, to which Temple alluded in his letter quoted previously. In answer to Joly's request that he find means to suppress all such books, Daniël replied that he favored the project and was ready to do it provided the French government would send agents to Holland to work under his direction. In the meantime he would make preparations for them at Amsterdam, Leyden, Utrecht, and other cities where he had relatives and friends in government. The French court sent a Monsieur Praslard, and the English government instructed Sir William Temple to assist this agent. Elsevier and Praslard then succeeded in having the States of Holland, and the authorities at Utrecht, Leyden, Amsterdam, and other cities, pass laws requiring booksellers possessing infamous books (designated by title) to bring them to the booksellers' gild hall, where they were paid for their stocks by Elsevier and Praslard acting for the French government. Elsevier pointed out that although the scheme worked well, all labor would be lost if the French government did not take similar measures in Liège, Cologne, Hamburg, Frankfurt, Nuremberg, Strasbourg, Geneva, Leipzig, and above all, in Flanders and Brabant, for otherwise it would mean that the lucrative trade in such books had merely been transferred from Dutchmen to dealers in the places mentioned. Some have questioned the propriety of Daniël in acting for a foreign government to suppress books, but his action cannot be viewed entirely apart from public policy. If it were fitting and proper for the Netherlands to placate France and England, then it was appropriate that Elsevier should do his part to further the policy. A sense of justice, as well as expediency, may have prompted his action. The anonymous printing of slanderous books was a profitable business. He steadily refused to participate in it, which was consistent with efforts to suppress it. He may have felt such books were unfair to the people slandered, as well as dangerous to the state and trade.

By 1680 Daniël was one of the famous publishers of Europe. In that year he was fifty-four. On several occasions he suffered from fevers which periodically struck Amsterdam. On 12 October, 1680, Graevius, a famous scholar, wrote Nicolaas Heinsius to say, 'Daniël Elsevier and five others in his household are ill with fever,' and on the fourteenth again wrote to Heinsius saying, 'We have received sad news; our old friend in common, Daniël Elsevier, died yesterday at noon.' 'The world of letters,' he added, 'has suffered a great loss.' Others expressed similar sentiments. John Locke wrote Thoynard that 'The death of Mr Elsevier is a public loss.' His death meant the end of the Amsterdam house. His great retail stock, the largest in Europe possibly, was sold, and also the stocks of his own publications which were on hand. His widow published several books after his death, but the Amsterdam establishment was finished by March, 1681. There remained only to carry on the great name of Elsevier those descendants at Leyden, who, it will be remembered, were ruining it with considerable efficiency.

7

The Elsevierian World

THUS far this halting narrative has been burdened with exactions of chronology, but having spun out the tale of Elsevierian years and laid the last printers to rest, there is opportunity to view them in perspective, to identify conditions permitting them to develop and flourish as they did. An important fact in Elsevierian history is that the family lived in a century when governments, to a remarkable extent, sought to order the lives of their peoples. It was the time of emergence of strong states under autocratic rulers. In Prussia the great elector easily reduced the Prussian Diet to impotence, suppressed the Estates of the Mark, Cleves, and Ravensberg with hardly less difficulty, and set up a centralized administration in which he was the absolute authority. In France, although there had been set-backs, despotism gained steadily from the reign of Henry IV through the regimes of Richelieu and Mazarin until the time when Louis XIV might logically sum up the situation by saying, 'L'état c'est moi.' In Russia, at the beginning of the century, feudal boyars were still the power in the land, but with the advent of the Romanoffs (1613) the rights of the Czars became undisputed, and nobles, bourgeoisie and serfs submitted increasingly to an autocratic form of government which still has great vogue in that country. In Scandinavian countries, also, strong, national autocracies developed.

The creation of such national, centralized states from debris of the feudal system was a difficult task, requiring strong measures. On the political side, free towns and small principalities were gobbled up, and parliamentary bodies were reduced to impotence. On the religious side, the idea of the divine right of kings had new interest and importance, and a state church, or at least strong state control over the Roman Catholic Church within the national borders, became common phenomena. On the economic side there were efforts to do away with special privileges of individual towns and bourgeois groups and to shape economic life in such a way that it increased the power of the sovereign. Increase in wealth and power of the state was the ultimate aim of regulation generally; individual regulations revealed various devices by which it was hoped to achieve the end. Laws were enacted against shoddy goods or short measure so that the country might win a reputation for quality goods. To assure healthy, prosperous industry, there were laws to prohibit underpaying workmen. Other laws sought to eliminate competition of foreign goods, to insure an ample flow of raw materials, to foster infant industry, and provide stocks of war materials. In brief, in its drive for power the state engendered the whole agglomeration of regulations which we know as mercantilism.

One phase of regulation of especial interest here was the granting of monopolies to individuals or groups, it being the theory that the crown would benefit from monopolies in two ways: first, by getting immediate revenue from their sale, and second, by creating a rich manufacture which could be tapped in future. The English crown endeavored to promote a war material industry by granting a monopoly for gathering salt petre and manufacturing gunpowder. For fifty years prior to 1635 the monopoly was mainly held by the Evelyn family. Privy councilors of Elizabeth and James held that the crown had regalian rights to salt petre, and the Evelyns were permitted to dig it anywhere, regardless of who owned the property. The Evelyn powder contract was renewed under Charles I, who also arranged to grant monopolies to a group of soap-makers, and a company of brick-makers. After 1630 a monopoly granted on alum brought considerable sums to his treasury. English monarchs granted patents for oversea trade as well as manufacture. A company of gentlemen adventurers received the right to trade into Hudson's Bay; groups were privileged to trade also into Moscovy, Greenland, Africa, the Indies, and other regions.

In the world of monopoly, chartered companies, and endless regulation shaped by ambitious princes, there were a few areas, such as Holland, where restriction was much less intense. In Holland, of course, the king had been eliminated, and development in the direction of the modern, centralized and bureaucratic state stopped. The Dutch Republic was in many ways a medieval survival. It is not meant to say there was not a great deal of government in trade in Holland also, but it was looser, less co-ordinated and centralized, and usually there were means of circumventing the rules. In the first part of the century there was, for example, a plethora of regulations in the provinces for trade in beer, but since these varied from province to province the net result was a prosperous interprovincial beer smuggling trade. The position of Holland as one of the less ordered islands in a sea of regulation had important bearing on the country's commerce, and incidentally on her book trade, for the Dutch showed remarkable ability to turn regulation in force in other lands to their own advantage. The intent of Cromwell's navigation laws was development of English trade; in some instances, they developed that of Holland instead. Ephraim Lipson in his *Economic History of England* points out that after passage of the acts the Dutch, who held undisputed ascendency in the Baltic, enjoyed more lucrative trade than before. Formerly they brought hemp and flax from Baltic ports to England where the materials were made into ropes, nets and sails. After passage of the laws, their ships were prohibited from carrying these products into that country. As an alternative, the Dutch carried raw materials to Holland and manufactured sails and cordage themselves. Subsequently, these finished products being now Dutch goods, were legally carried into England where their sale proved more profitable than had hemp and flax. English manufacture suffered, and numbers of English workmen were thrown out of employment. As another example, Spain restricted trade with her colonies to her own subjects. Actually there were not enough Spanish goods or Spanish merchants to satisfy colonial needs. By subterfuge, usually by working in the name of a Spanish national, the Dutch (and others) gained access to the famished oversea markets and gathered a large part of the trade into their own hands. Political and religious restrictions in other lands, forcing artisans and merchants into exile, also benefited the Netherlands. Calvinists from the southern Netherlands, Huguenots from France, Jews from Spain and Portugal, Puritans from England, all contributed wealth and skill to make Holland great.

These are instances of how, generally speaking, Holland turned paternalistic efforts of her neighbors to her own advantage. In the narrower area of the book trade, regulation also benefited Dutch merchants. Two forms of foreign regulation came to their aid: first, regulation of ideas, and second, regulation of books as articles of commerce. Incidentally, regulation of ideas should be recognized as merely part of the effort of a despot to make his state strong, a necessary counterpart of mercantilist economic policy. Religious ideas which might weaken the state either by creating hostile parties, or questioning the divine right of the king, were eliminated. Mental and moral fibre of the people was protected by banning salacious images, regardless of whether they were painted, acted, or written. The prince protected his majesty by eliminating libels against himself, family, servants, or friends, regardless of whether the libels were printed, sung, or passed about in manuscript. It is worth remembering it was not the medium, but the idea which was singled out for suppression, and hence to speak of censorship of books is to give a distorted view of the situation.

Restrictions on books as articles of commerce exhibited all characteristics evident in restrictions on trade generally. Analogous to granting monopolies to manufacturers was the granting of exclusive privileges to print certain books, such as were granted to the king's printer. In the early years of the century James I gave Robert Barker the title of 'King's Printer' and granted him the monopoly to print, among other things, the royal statutes. In the same reign, John Norton held a royal patent to print certain books in Latin, Greek and Hebrew, and later also obtained the patent to print grammars. Another printer, William Hilliard, had the right to engrave and print the king's picture. The great monopolistic body in the printing industry was the Company of Stationers. Like individuals, it held monopolies on specific works. Under James I it held the right to print Psalters and primers. As the Evelyns were protected in their rights by laws forbidding unauthorized persons to dig salt petre or to make gunpowder, so likewise no one might erect a printing press or let any premises for the carrying on of printing, nor could any joiner or carpenter build a press without giving notice to the Stationers' Company. John Lilburne termed the Stationers ' . . . that insufferable, unjust, and tyrannical Monopoly of Printing,' adding that they were 'invested with an Arbitrary unlimmitted *Power*, even by a generall Ordinance of Parliament, to print, divulge and disperse whatsoever Books, Pamphlets, and Libells they please, . . . ' Analogous to monopolies granted for general trade in foreign parts, the Stationers' Company obtained the royal privilege for printing and importing books into Ireland. In France, the Compagnie de Morbihan, created by Richelieu, enjoyed such rights as the monopoly of all trade with the East and West Indies and with northern Europe, the right to exploit the fisheries, to discover and exploit mines, to seize beggars when workmen were needed, and in addition, the privilege to print and sell books. From such examples it is evident that much regulation of publishing was identical with commercial regulation generally. As has been said, Dutch publishers benefited both from regulation of commerce and regulation of ideas. The way in which they benefited from foreign thought-control is obvious. The writings of Huguenots, screeds against Mazarin, the literature of Jansenism, the arguments of English royalists, of Cromwellians, and, in short, all literatures banned in their homelands because of dangerous ideas expressed, were printed in Holland. In the identical way in which the Dutch found their way into other markets famished by restriction, they found their way into book markets undersupplied because of thought control, or monopoly. The printing of English Bibles illustrates how the Dutch benefited from too strict control of industry. Throughout the seventeenth century, with some interruption, the printing of Bibles was the exclusive privilege of the royal printers, descendants of the original patentee, Christopher Barker, and of the two universities. In 1671-2 John Fell, zealous to place the Oxford Press on a secure footing, proposed to utilize the University privilege to print Bibles which had been temporarily relinquished. The king's printers, apprehensive of the University's design, complained there was little money in printing Bibles. The reason given for the sad state of affairs was 'the Hollanders continuall poureing in vast numbers of Bibles,' so that they sold not a tenth part of what they formerly did. Actual records of English Bibles printed in Holland are fairly numerous. Tomas Loof, Amsterdam printer, had sixteen hundred such volumes in 1641. In 1644 Hugo Fitz, merchant of Amsterdam, entered an agreement with Jan Frederickszoon Stam and Thomas Craffort for printing six thousand English Bibles. Joseph Athias, widely known printer of Amsterdam, boasted that 'for several years I myself printed more than a million Bibles for England and Scotland. There is no plow boy or servant girl there without one.' In 1670 the States of Holland granted him the exclusive privilege to print English Bibles for a period of fifteen years. Similarly the Dutch printed works in short supply in France. An historian of the Dutch book trade remarks that one of the most lucrative branches of the trade was printing French works and selling them again in France.

Exiles and refugees gave impetus to book and printing trades as they did to other commerce. Large numbers of bookmen were from France and southern Netherlands, and others were from England. Spanish and Portuguese Jews offer a striking illustration of how exiles promoted trade. In the seventeenth century and until 1732 there were three hundred and eighteen Jewish printers in Amsterdam, almost all of whom were of families exiled from Spain and Portugal. Of these, the best known are the Rabbi printers Menasseh ben Israel and Joseph Athias, but many others conducted business on a large scale, and Amsterdam became the European center for Hebrew printing. A commentary on Amsterdam's position is the fact that in 1685, after deliberation, the city government of Breslau decided not to establish a printing press, because 'in Holland in Amsterdam there are three important Jewish presses from which books are brought to Danzig and Memel by sea. In this way the Jews of Poland and Lithuania are furnished with these books.' A glimpse of the Danzig trade is revealed by an agreement signed at Amsterdam by the widow of Justus Bake, Laurens Bake, Willem Blaeu, and the Rabbi Meijer Frankel at Danzig whereby Frankel was to be furnished five hundred copies of a Yiddish Bible which he was to sell in Danzig and Poland. The contrast between the size of editions of Jewish books and the size of the Jewish population makes obvious what a large proportion of Amsterdam printings were intended for export. In 1645 there were not two thousand Sephardic Jews in the city, yet in that year Menasseh ben Israel contracted to print four thousand copies of the Mishnah. Two years earlier

Emmanuel Benvenist had printed eight thousand copies of the Hebrew prayerbook. In 1694 David Tartas contracted to print ten thousand copies of a prayerbook, which would have provided at least one copy for every Jew in Amsterdam. Jews all over Europe bought books produced in the Dutch city, and the term 'Amsterdam edition,' was a synonym for a reliable, well-printed text. Other nationals also established presses in Holland: Swedish Bibles were printed at Amsterdam, and the Pilgrim Fathers had a press at Leyden. About 1640 Armenians settled in Amsterdam and there were printed the first Armenian hymn books (1666), the first Armenian Bible (1666), and the first ritual (1667). In the same decade Comenius was instrumental in establishing a Czech press in the city.

The book trade in Holland, then, prospered for the same reasons other branches of Dutch trade prospered. It utilized skills and foreign connections of exiled workmen, manufactured a superior product for export, and took advantage of dearth of goods in other countries resulting from excessive regulation. In the case of the book trade Holland was but one of a number of regions profiting by restrictions on trade in more powerful countries. Daniël Elsevier pointed out that if the French government wished to prevent publication of books it thought harmful government must control not only printing in Holland but also in the Spanish Netherlands, Liège, and German principalities, since otherwise the only effect would be to transfer trade in such books from Holland to her neighbors. Later Accarias de Serrione observed that 'if today the publication of a book is prohibited in Holland, tomorrow an edition printed at Liège, or in Maastricht, or in any one of a number of places, is on sale.'

In another sense also the book trade resembled industry generally. To a large degree the Dutch imported raw materials and exported a finished product. Contemporaries remarked that Holland had no native timber and yet the greatest shipbuilding industry in Europe; very few sheep, but a major share in the cloth trade. Development of the book trade was analogous in the sense that texts (the raw materials of publishing) of French, German, English, and Italian works were printed in Holland and sold again in the countries of origin.

Around the printing trade developed other flourishing industries: type casting, engraving, and paper making. When the Oxford University Press wanted oriental types it was from Holland they were gotten, and there are records extant of English printers voyaging to Holland to buy types. It is said that by 1700 half the types in use in England came from Dutch letter foundries. The paper-making industry arose at the time of the founding of the republic. During the wars with Spain it was difficult for the Dutch to get paper from the countries south of them, and Leicester, in 1586, authorized Hans van Aelst and Johan Lupaert to establish two mills. A French refugee, Martin Orges, established a paper mill in Gelders in 1613, and from the mill developed the great paper industry of the province. By 1697 there were forty paper mills in the village of Zaandam, and in 1721 it was noted that there were at least an equal number around Wormerveer. Before 1682 Dutch paper makers developed the cylindrical device for macerating pulp materials, since known as a 'Hollander.' In 1725 a German paper maker, speaking of the invention, said that 'The Hollander in Freiburg furnishes in one day as much pulp as eight stamper-holes [the older method] do in eight days.' In 1697 a German architect interested in paper mills visited Zaandam. 'Beyond a doubt,' he later wrote, 'much better paper is made in Holland than is made in Germany.' In addition to Zaandam there were mills at Leyden, Gouda, and Groningen. Not only was quality good, but the quantity relatively large, it being said that toward the end of the seventeenth century one hundred thousand reams were sold at Amsterdam in one day. Probably by that time the Dutch surpassed the French paper trade in volume. In addition, large quantities of French-made paper were imported and a large proportion re-exported, so that Amsterdam became an entrepôt for French paper. An indication of the important place of Holland in the French trade is that paper made at French mills was frequently watermarked with the arms of the city of Amsterdam, and in the latter half of the century a considerable part of the capital invested in those mills was Dutch.

The foregoing remarks sketch, however briefly, the relation of the book trade to trade in general. Certain facts, in turn, indicate the relations of Elseviers to the book trade. Obviously there were areas of the Dutch printing industry where Elseviers never entered or where their efforts were negligible. They were not concerned, for example, with the business of printing corantos (newspapers) and newsbooks, although seventeenth-century Amsterdam was the newspaper center of Europe. The first English newspapers were printed in Holland in 1620 and 1621, the first French newspapers were printed there in the same years, and Dutch and German corantos were also published. As might be expected in a seafaring nation, a flourishing trade developed in maps, atlases, narrations of voyages, and books on navigation. Amsterdam was not only the center of sea trade, but also for books about the sea. The house of Van Keulen was famous for its correct and elaborate sea-charts, considered the finest in the Netherlands. Their *Zeefakkel*, or *Torch of the Sea*, was published with English, French, Spanish, and Italian text, and was so well known that its title, translated into various languages, was the accepted name for a book of navigation charts: in England, the *Great and Little Sea-Torches*, in France, the *Flambeaux de la Mer*. In the seventeenth century English seamen largely depended upon Dutch charts and pilot books. Lucas Waghenaer's *Spiegel der Seevaert* (1584–5) was translated in England as *The Mariner's Mirror*, but the name of the Dutch publisher persisted. Throughout the eighteenth century in England a book of charts and sailing directions was known as a 'wagoner.' Two Dutch names which come immediately to our minds when maps and atlases are mentioned are Blaeu and Hondius.

Wide-ranging Dutch seamen provided voluminous first-hand material for travel books. Towards the end of the sixteenth century the voyages of Jan Huygen van Lin- schoten were published and his adventures were quickly translated into French, German and English. An account of the voyage of Cornelis Houtman appeared in 1598, and the many descriptions of the countries of the East by Olfert Dapper were published throughout the last quarter of the century. Johannes Nieuhof's travels in Brazil and China also appeared in the latter part of the century, and Arnoldus Montanus' work on the wonders of the East was published in 1650. These are only a few of many published voyages and travel books. Some publishers, like Cornelis Claeszoon, specialized in such literature. Claeszoon published the voyages of Gerrit de Veer in 1598, 1599 and 1609; the voyages of Drake and Cavendish

in 1598; Cornelis Houtman in 1598 and 1609; that of
Walter Raleigh and Lawrence Kemys in 1598 and 1605;
Jacob van Neck in 1600, 1602, 1608; Olivier van Noort,
1602; Pierre de Marees, 1602; Laurens Bicker and Jacob
van Heemskerk in 1603. He published many of these in
French, producing folio editions of voyages of De Veer,
Houtman, Van Neck, Van Noort, and Marees; Latin
editions of De Veer, Houtman, Linschoten; and a German
edition of Van Noort. In the literature for and of the sea
the Elseviers had practically no part. Neither did they
participate in the chap-book trade, and popular reading on
a somewhat higher plane they left untouched as well. Booksellers had translated the *Arcadias* of Sannazzaro and Sidney
which proved immensely popular and inspired numerous
insipid Dutch imitations. D'Urfé's *Astrée* was taken to the
Dutch heart, appearing in both French and Dutch translation, and exercising profound influence on Dutch writers;
but neither Sidney nor Sannazzaro, nor D'Urfé's romance
was printed by Elseviers. A profitable line of publishing
was singing books. The *Singing Goddess* went through five
editions; the *Amsterdam Pleasure Festival*, ten editions; *Jolly
Company*, seven editions. Seventeenthcentury Dutch *burgers*
remained sentimentally attached to the medieval literature,
or its derivatives, which had been popular with their forefathers. *Floris and Blanchefleur* went through six editions in the
Netherlands in the seventeenth century; *Oerson and Valen-
tine*, six editions; *Griselda*, three editions; *Beautiful Helena*,
eight editions. There were also many editions of *Karel and
Elegast, The Victorious Diederyck van Elseten, The Knight, Helias,
Seghelyn van Jerusalem*, and *Reynard the Fox*. The Elseviers
paid slight attention to the profit in romances or singing
books; they were printers for the educated and scholarly.

Pursuing further the search for a proper perspective on

the Elseviers, it is apparent their house was not a bright star on a dark night, but one of a galaxy of fine printing houses. In prosperous, stable industries, individual firms are also stable and long-enduring. The Elseviers were in the book business under their own name for about one hundred and thirty-two years. Their contemporaries, the Van Waesberghes, were in business from 1557 to 1869, the Wetsteins from 1676 to 1755, the Enschedés from 1703 to the present day, the Hackius family from 1608 to 1702, the Van Ravesteyns from 1611 to 1695, the House of Luchtmans from 1683 to 1848. Travelers thought the Elsevier Leyden establishment one of the sights worth seeing, but other presses also were sought by discriminating visitors. In his account of his travels in Germany and Holland Claude Joly said that while in Holland (27 August, 1646), 'I went to see the Blaeu press which is considered the best in Europe. As a matter of fact, there were ten presses which worked incessantly in a long, low room, at one end of which was a room for men of letters and proof-readers, and at the other end were arranged all the geographical and other plates, for it is he who printed the great Atlas and almost all the beautifully decorated maps which we have. There also are all kinds of types, including those for oriental languages, which have been cast in his establishment . . . ' Eighteen years later another visitor, Filips von Zesen, speaks of there being nine presses for letterpress and six presses to print engravings in the Blaeu establishment. He described the place in great detail, being especially struck by the array of copper plates for maps and atlases which he says 'certainly cost a ton of gold.' Although the Elsevier establishment was well known, there are few admiring descriptions of it such as these.

It is enlightening also to compare the size of Elsevier

editions and retail stock with those of contemporaries. When Daniël Elsevier died in 1681 his stock contained eight thousand Latin works, not counting duplicates, and five thousand works in modern languages. More than forty years earlier (in 1638) Hendrick Laurenszoon had issued a two-hundred page catalogue containing eight thousand titles. In 1699 the stock of Henry Wetstein, erstwhile apprentice of Daniël, contained, exclusive of duplicates, six thousand Latin books and three thousand in modern languages. The catalogue of Blaeu's stock comprised a good three hundred closely printed pages. Concerning the size of printings, it appears editions of twenty-five hundred or three thousand copies were not uncommon with the Elseviers, but other printers, aiming at a wider clientele, printed in larger numbers. In 1644 a six-thousand-copy edition of the English Bible was printed in Holland. Editions of Hebrew and Yiddish books were notably large. A Yiddish Bible was issued in an edition of six thousand three hundred, and records indicate three thousand, four thousand and ten thousand copies of other Jewish works were issued.

Like the Elseviers, other houses did business in several Dutch cities. The Van Ravesteyns had establishments at both Amsterdam and Leyden, and Daniël van Gaesbeek, his relatives and heirs (1655–1708) also maintained establishments in both cities. Of twenty-eight Van Waesberghes in the book trade, nine were established at Amsterdam, sixteen at Rotterdam, one in Amsterdam and Danzig, one at Amsterdam and Utrecht, and one at Breda. The Elseviers, not content with a Dutch trade, established connections throughout Europe. They visited the Frankfurt fair, sold books in Italy, London, Paris, and French provincial cities, had working arrangements with

French and English dealers, a branch in Denmark, and some traffic with, and perhaps an agent in Sweden. They were not unique in this respect. The foreign trade of the Huguetans, French émigré booksellers of Amsterdam, was such that, according to contemporaries, there was not a principality or city in the whole of Europe where the Huguetans did not have agents, clerks, or warehouses. An agreement (dated 1694) between Marc, Jean, and Pierre Huguetan has been preserved which lists debtors to the firm; among those owing are 'Sr Delgas of London and Oxford, 10.000,00 guilders; Olenschlager at Frankfort, 14.107,10 guilders; in our shop at Leipzig, 4.451,14; in Livorno 17.522,40 guilders; in Lisbon and Alicante 10.029,10.' It is stated also that they are owed: in Italy 34.879,90 francs; in Germany 14.344,11 marks; in England 902.13 pounds sterling; in Portugal 4,823,82 Rees; in Holland, France, Spain, and Flanders 37.801,14 guilders. Other facts indicative of the Europe-wide connections of Dutch printers have been preserved. The heirs of Joan Blaeu delivered to Moses Pitt, sometime a large scale bookseller at Oxford and London, five hundred copies of the *Opera Theologica* of Hugo de Groot, these copies bearing the imprint of Pitt. In 1663 Jan Jacobs Schipper of Amsterdam entered into an agreement with two book-sellers of Lyons to print the *Concilium omnium Generalium et provincialium collectio regia*. Aronold Colom, printer of Amsterdam, agreed to print a pilot-book of the Mediter-ranean for John Tuthill of Yarmouth. The executors of the estate of Johannes Janssonius (died 1664) listed, among other book catalogues of the deceased printer, catalogues of stocks held by Janssonius in shops at Frank-furt, Danzig, Stockholm, Copenhagen, and Berlin, as well as unsold stocks at Königsberg, Geneva, and Lyons.

European-wide trading in books was again only a counter-part of Europe-wide trading in other commodities. Professor J. H. Kernkamp has pointed out that an Armenian press at Amsterdam would not have been feasible without already existing extensive Dutch trade connections in the Levant. The firm of Louis de Geer is a favored example of the wide-ranging activities of Dutch merchants. The firm armed and equipped many of the armies employed in the thirty-years' war; Mansfeld and Brunswick bought considerable quantities of weapons from him, and he largely financed the campaigns of Gustavus Adolphus (1630–2). In 1616 he asked permission of the States General to send weapons for a thousand men to La Rochelle, and made considerable shipments of arms to France in later years. In 1617 he shipped weapons to England, and in 1621 contracted to sell four thousand muskets and four thousand harnesses to the British government. He secured control of the Swedish copper trade, laid the foundations of Sweden's heavy industry, and was the mainstay of Swedish finance. Dr Bernard Vlekke points out that in Sweden's war with Denmark for control of the Baltic (1645) De Geer 'assembled a navy in Dutch ports, equipped it with guns from his storehouses, manned it with a Dutch crew, entrusted the command to a Dutch admiral. Flying the Swedish flag, this fleet sailed for the Baltic and defeated the Danish navy which by the way, was largely composed of hired Dutch auxiliaries.' All of De Geer's enterprises were not on so large a scale. In 1626 he sent two ships to load coal in Scotland which was sold in a French port, where a cargo (probably salt) was loaded for Amsterdam. He also sent ships to trade in the Mediterranean, and on a yet smaller scale, maintained a retail store in Stockholm where he sold small hardware and kitchen utensils, his daughters waiting on the customers. De Geer was outstanding, but nonetheless a typical Dutch merchant. By the middle of the century the places where his compatriots were trading was a roll-call of lands and cities of the known world. Of an estimated twenty thousand seafaring ships in Europe at that time, between fifteen thousand and sixteen thousand were Dutch. Activities of Dutch printers in foreign lands were analogous, though of course on a smaller scale, to those of merchants like De Geer.

In their mode of operation and the scale of their enterprises the Elseviers were of their time. Idiosyncrasies they displayed were traits they also shared with contemporaries. There have been complaints that the Elseviers fell short at times of wholly commendable conduct; specifically, they were stingy. As was mentioned heretofore, Gronovius was charged by the Elseviers fifteen *stuivers* postage for transporting a letter which actually cost them nothing to deliver. The printers charged the same scholar the cost of transporting a book he needed in preparing a new edition of Livy for the Elseviers themselves. Finally, there is the regrettable story of the cruel treatment of the children of Cluver. But such lapses into avariciousness were not uncommon. It was said that Willem Janszoon Blaeu sought favor with the Catholics to get the business of printing Catholic books. Vossius, writing in 1638, said of him, 'This man sets more store by his own good than by the general good; he is more concerned for gold than for honor, and thinks of nothing but profit. He now says that nothing brings him a profit outside of his maps and that now he can annex the trade in mass-books and such like things, especially so as he uses the name of a Cologne printer on the title-page.' Travelers in Holland observed hordes of beggars let loose upon the streets in the evening. They were not unemployed, but were paid so little by parsimonious employers they eked out an existence by begging at the end of the day. Owen Feltham in his *Batavia* observed the Dutch were not 'so nice-conscienced, but that they can turn out Religion to let in Policy,' and added that love of gain was as natural to them as water to a goose.

The Elseviers might also be considered unethical since they were familiar with all shady tricks and devices of bookselling. One finds their new editions to be merely old editions with a few pages added. A new title-page was sometimes given an old book, or two old books were bound together as a new volume. But such publishing practices are by no means dead. We have our share of 'newly revised editions,' in which changes are trivial, and sometimes printed from the old plates; we have frequently examples of government documents reprinted by private individuals and advertised as new works. As has been pointed out also the tone of business in this seafaring nation in those days was set by oversea traders, and what their methods were is indicated by Jacques Savary, who relates an incident in the history of competition in the East India trade. A French ship had the misfortune to be caught on the way home from the East Indies by a Dutch East Indiaman. The captain and the lieutenant of the French vessel had their heads bound with cords until their eyes started out of the sockets, and the two unfortunate officers were then stabbed to death. Sixteen French sailors were hanged and the rest burned on the soles of their feet. Methods were gentler in the book trades, but the more one contemplates the conduct of others in the era, seamen, merchants, manufacturers, most Elseviers emerge as upright gentlemen. Their successes and shortcomings were those of their time, an era in which Dutch trade was the most extensive and powerful of all European countries.

In the century succeeding, Dutch commerce was on the decline, at first a relative decline, and later an actual decline, and the book trade suffered with the rest. The great names in eighteenth-century printing history are not Dutch. Accarias de Serrione, writing in the latter half of the eighteenth century, said that 'formerly the Dutch booksellers drove an active commerce with foreign lands. Today they have only a passive commerce. Formerly the foreigners purchased Dutch editions; today Holland pays the journeymen who worked, for example, on the various editions of the Encyclopedias which have rapidly multiplied, and for all the other foreign works which are circulated daily in Holland, and which the Dutch, fifty years ago, would not have failed promptly to reprint; today the editions of Liège and Maastricht inundate Holland. Hardly a Dutch bookseller dares go to the expense of printing an original edition for fear a pirated edition will deprive him of the profits . . . ' A great Dutch printing house of the eighteenth century might be more difficult to explain, but viewing the Elseviers against the seventeenth-century background of commercial and industrial strength their development seems a natural one. Shrewd and intelligent traders, for the greater part, they contributed their share to the pre-eminence of Holland.

8

The Elseviers as Printers and Publishers

THE bibliography and typography of the Elseviers and their imitators have been covered in detail and unusually well by Willems, Berghman and Rahir. Berghman reproduced typographical ornaments, and Rahir, in the catalogue of his library, reproduced not only printing ornaments of Elseviers, but those of contemporaries who imitated them. But although bibliography and typography have already been well presented, it is permissible to attempt some generalizations on Elsevier publishing as a whole. Considering all Elsevier printings or issues, the volumes of Leyden, Amsterdam, and the few at Utrecht and The Hague, it is obvious the favorite subject matter was religion and theology; the next field in popularity was law and politics; the third, classics; and the fourth, French plays and belles lettres. The texts varied in quality. The Elseviers were not scholars and relatively few even well educated; they therefore depended upon proof-readers and authors themselves to insure correct texts. If an author were negligent in proof-reading, or if proofs were read at a distance from the press and communication difficult, faulty text resulted. This sometimes happened despite the best efforts of printers. When Nicolaas Heinsius complained there were typographical errors in his edition of Paterculus, Daniël Elsevier replied,

142

'I am astonished you still have found errors in the Velleius, for the proofs have been read by three readers and then by yourself. If after that, one doesn't succeed in printing correctly, the attempt had better be given up.' In the Elsevier era the tradition of scholar proof-readers had largely passed away. Aldus had many scholars attached to his establishment; Erasmus read proof for Froben at Basle, and Rabelais read for Étienne Dolet and Gryphius at Lyon. The names and some records of Elsevier readers have survived but the men were generally not notable. An exception must be made in the case of Johan de Laet who read proof at Leyden. De Laet was a member of the Synod of Dordrecht, and a director of the West Indies Company. His description of the West Indies and other writings on America are well known to historians. He compiled for the Elseviers the 'Republics' on the Netherlands, France, Spain, Portugal, Turkey, the Empire of the Great Mogol, and Poland-Lithuania-Prussia-Livonia. He also conducted a written feud with Grotius on the origin of the American Indians, and edited a volume on architecture. But there were not sufficient men like De Laet to make the press a scholarly establishment like that of Aldus.

Inevitably there was an occasional faulty edition, but in general texts were well edited and reliable. Alphonse Willems, trained as a classicist and with first-hand acquaintance with Elsevier classics, declared that for the most part the editions left nothing to be desired, and in some cases, as with the Virgil of 1676, the texts were models of correctness which, up until his time, had not been surpassed. Willems pointed out also that whereas French and Italian books published in Holland in the seventeenth century gained a reputation for being replete with errors, Elsevier texts in these languages were quite satisfactory. In a number of instances their reprints were better than original issues.

Many Elsevier volumes appeared without imprint, or with a fictitious imprint, but the number of these is not nearly as great as was thought before publication of Willems' bibliography. Willems identified the great majority of books issued by the printers without revealing their identity, and he deduced the basic reason why they were so issued. He found about two-thirds of the volumes in this class gave no indication of printer, and the remaining third gave false or fictitious printers. Jansenist publications had wholly fictitious imprints, the Elseviers affixing the names of imaginary printers at Cologne and Liège to such works. In France Jansenists were often accused of being Calvinists, and publication of their works in Calvinist Holland would have lent color to the charge. Other Catholic religious works sometimes bore simply the imprint *Lugduni*, instead of the usual *Lugduni Batavorum*, thus conveying the impression they were printed at Lyons rather than Leyden. The Elseviers also often remained anonymous, or pseudonymous, when issuing political works. On the one hand, Saumaise's defense of Charles I was issued three times, twice in 1649 and once in 1652, without the Elseviers putting their name to the book, obviously to avoid displeasing Commonwealth men. To avoid the wrath of English loyalists, on the other hand, Louis Elsevier published anonymously (in 1651) Milton's defense of the English people, a reply to Saumaise, and the following year printed an anonymous reply to Milton. John Selden's *Mare Clausum*, a work asserting his Britannic Majesty's dominion over the seas, was issued, in 1636, without indication of Elseviers as printer both because the book might offend their Dutch countrymen, and because Bonaventura and Abraham perhaps felt shamefaced about it, since three years earlier they had reprinted Grotius' *Mare Liberum*, which asserted the contrary doctrine of freedom of the seas. Similarly, to avoid giving offense to compatriots, the same printers published anonymously the accounts of the Dutch-Spanish war written by Bentivoglio, Conestaggio, and Strada, all biased in favor of Spain.

In some cases, when Elseviers reprinted a work first printed by another, they appropriated not only text but the original publisher's imprint. Sometimes they preferred pseudonymity to anonymity. Johannes and Daniël at Leyden used the name 'Jean Sambix.' The Amsterdam house preferred 'Jacques le Jeune,' but also used, on different occasions, the imprints: Cologne, J. du Païs; Cologne, P. du Marteau; Amsterdam, P. le Grand, and Amsterdam, Antoine Michel. Reprints of French plays and other items of belles lettres usually were given simply the imprint 'Jouxte (or Suivant) la copie de Paris.' Of all books issued without imprint or with fictitious imprint, French plays and belles lettres were by far the largest class, comprising more than fifty per cent of titles so issued. About sixteen per cent of such publications were political writings, and an equal percentage was theological works. The remaining volumes were concerned with miscellaneous subjects.

The Elsevierian reputation for printing has chiefly depended upon books in small format. To many, an Elsevier is synonymous with a small book. As a matter of fact, if one considers Elsevier printings and publications as a whole including all issued at Leyden, Amsterdam, The Hague and Utrecht (but excluding theses printed at

Leyden), it is found only about forty-two per cent of the titles are duodecimos; and there are well over a hundred folios and about two hundred twenty-five octavos. But duodecimos made such a reputation they are now considered the characteristic Elsevier publication.

Present-day historians of printing are inclined to dismiss our printers with a brief, perfunctory treatment; but if they were viewed not primarily as typographers, but as skilful, competent publishers specializing in small books, interest in them might revive. As was pointed out earlier, their little 'Republics' constituted a series, the prototype of the *Chronicles of America*, *World Classics*, or *Home University Library*; and publication of the duodecimo volumes gave them a distinguished place among printers who have endeavored to give the public good books at low prices. The truth of Samuel Johnson's well-worn observation, 'books that you may carry to the fire and hold readily in your hand, are the most useful after all,' was apparent to many before him. Aldus was among the first to perceive it, and the publishers of Penguin Books, Bantam Books, and volumes in similar format are the latest.

The Elseviers' part in the history of small, cheap books is so important it is worth recalling the main facts in the development of that kind of publishing. Aldus published the first of his classics in small format in 1501 'at a very reasonable price and accessible to all fortunes,' as Renouard observes. In that year appeared first the small Aldine Virgil, and then the satires of Juvenal and Persius. In the dedication to the latter volume Aldus explains why he issued the books. He says that 'We have printed, and are now publishing, the Satires of Juvenal and Persius in a very small *format* so that they may more conveniently be held in the hand and learned by the heart (not to speak of being read) by everyone . . . ' He continued to issue such books for many years, and after his death his son and grandson published them until the eighth decade of the sixteenth century. The books were successful from the beginning and gave rise to a host of imitators and forgeries. Printers at Lyon were notably assiduous in making capital of the new venture. Possibly in the very year the first small Aldine classic appeared (the Virgil, 1501), an imitation was published at Lyon. There is evidence to show Lyonnaise imitations sold faster than Venetian originals. Among many Lyonnaise printers who imitated small Aldines were the Giunti and Sebastian Gryphius. Parisian printers also adopted the new idea. Simon de Colines issued the *Odes* of Horace in 1539 and Martial's *Epigrams* in 1544; Geoffroy Tory, Michael Vascosan, and Robert Estienne also published small, cheap editions of Latin and Greek classics. Nearer home to the Elseviers, Plantin issued a large number of classics in small format. When the Elseviers, then, issued good books cheaply they followed a policy that had proved profitable to printers for generations, but the Elseviers issued more titles, probably in larger editions, and disposed of them through a Europe-wide sales system.

The first duodecimo classic was published in 1629 by Bonaventura and Abraham; the series grew rapidly, being received by the learned world with mixed emotions. Nicolaas Heinsius wrote Gronovius (1651) to say, 'The Dupuy brothers wish your Livy had been printed in larger format. They say the small types are a continual subject of complaint by scholars of their city.' Gronovius confessed that 'I myself could have wished my Livy had appeared in another format. I have already received a similar opinion from Germany, and that from the mouth of a prince; but try to make men listen to reason who have nothing else in their heads but the love of gain, who serve us not as useful counselors but as simple mechanics.'

As in the case of the Aldine classics, the success of Elsevier duodecimos brought out a rash of imitators. Willems lists at least three hundred and fifty-two books issued in Holland and two hundred nineteen in Brussels in imitation of Elsevier duodecimos before 1680; and these, he makes clear, are a selection of what he might have listed. In the catalogue of his collection Rahir listed about thirteen hundred and fifty imitations of Elsevier duodecimos, as against only about six hundred and seventy-five actually printed by Elseviers. Not only format, but Elsevier ornaments, aegipans, grotesques, hollyhocks, and spheres, were reproduced with varying degrees of skill. At Leyden in 1651 there were eight presses in operation (in addition to that of Abraham and Bonaventura), and at least seven of the eight printers, Jan Maire, Philip de Croy, Severyn Mathys, Frans Hacke, Joris Abrahams, Abraham Commelin, and Willem Christaens printed imitation Elseviers. At Amsterdam almost all printers were their imitators, including Johan Blaeu, Johannes Janssonius, Johannes J. van Waesberghe, and Abraham Wolfgang. At The Hague, Johannes and Daniël Steucker, Adrien Vlecq and Adrien Moetjens printed 'Elseviers;' at Gouda, Willem van der Hoeve; at Brussels, many printers, including such well-known men as François Foppens, Philippe Vleugart, Lambert Marchant, and Eugène Fricx. Outside the Netherlands imitations were issued at Paris, Rouen, and Liège. Elseviers, then, deserve an important place in the history of good books published at low prices. They not only influenced contemporaries, but those who came after. In the middle eighteenth century the scholar and bibliophile Nicolas Lenglet-Dufresnoy became alarmed that Elsevier duodecimo classics were becoming scarcer every year. He conceived the idea of reprinting them in small, handy format similar to the original issues. A group of Parisian printers agreed to publish them as a joint venture. The first of the new series, a volume containing the works of Catullus, Tibullus and Propertius, appeared in 1743; Sallust was published in 1744; Virgil, Cornelius Nepos and Lucian in 1745. Commencing with 1755 the volumes were published by Joseph Gérard Barbou, who was succeeded first by his nephew and then by others. Incidentally, it is interesting to note the first Barbou about whom anything is known was a printer at Lyons, who issued in that city in 1538 an edition of the works of Clement Marot, using italic types and a small octavo format after the manner of Aldine classics. Volumes continued to appear as late as 1810, the series comprising seventy-six duodecimo volumes at that time. Since Lenglet-Dufresnoy originally conceived the series as a continuation, or revivification of Elsevier duodecimos, it is permissible to say Elsevier influence was directly felt in publishing as late as 1810. Another manifestation of their influence is that in 1794, one hundred and fourteen years after Daniël died, there was published in England a duodecimo edition of John Locke's *The Conduct of the Understanding* with the imprint, 'London, printed for Daniel Elsevier junior, 1794.' With exception of the Aldine house, it is doubtful if another publisher made such an impression on the cheap book trade as did these printers.

The Elseviers have always had detractors, but for over a hundred years after they ceased publishing their adherents far outnumbered their critics, and they do not entirely deserve the neglect accorded them later. In the seventeenth century the great majority of those interested in books, even their enemies, conceded them to be fine printers. In 1650, when the Leyden house printed the works of Jean Guez de Balzac, that elegant gentleman wrote a letter replete with extravagant compliments. To be printed by Elseviers, he said, was to take rank among consuls and senators of Rome, to mingle with the Ciceros and Sallusts. 'I have been made a part of the immortal republic,' he exclaims. 'I have been received in the society of demi-gods. In effect, we all live together at Leyden under the same roof. Thanks to you, sometimes I am a neighbor of Pliny; sometimes I find myself beside Seneca, sometimes above Tacitus and Livy.' Thirteen years later Daniël Elsevier consented to print the poetry of Gilles Ménage, and in recognition of the signal favor Ménage included in the poems one in praise of Elseviers. 'Gods and Goddesses, what do I see,' he exclaims, 'My verses printed with Elsevier types. O elegant and exquisite types, O gracious and charming volume. The delicate letters equal pitch in blackness, the paper yields nothing to snow in whiteness. Thus gotten up the book attracts and holds the reader in spite of himself. The types lend to my verses charms they do not possess ... ' Ménage's compliments reach their most elegant stage when the author exclaims, ' ... Elsevier, my sweet glory, ... the friends of learning value and seek your charming productions; book lovers throng to your shop; because of you poets will transmit the name of Elsevier from age to age.' The fame of the volumes extended to England, and when Sir Thomas Browne died, in 1682, he desired by his will that 'on my coffin when in the grave I desire may be deposited in its leather case or coffin my Elzevir's Horace,

'Comes Viae Vitaeque dulcis et utilis,' worn out with and by me.' Nearly a hundred years later, in 1776, the Abbé de Fontenai observed the Elseviers 'have made Holland celebrated for printing, through an elegance of type which the most famous printers of Europe have never been able to attain, either before or since.' He adds that the charm of the types lies 'in the clearness, delicacy, and perfect uniformity of the letters, and in their very close fitting to each other.' The reputation for typographic excellence persisted into the nineteenth century. Charles H. Timperley, himself a journeyman printer, in his *Encyclopaedia of Literary and Typographical Anecdote* (1842) remarked, 'The Elzevier editions have long and deservedly been esteemed for the clearness, delicacy and perfect equality of the characters, for their close position together on a solid and very white paper, and the excellence of the presswork.' Timperley perhaps merely repeated traditional phrases without too extensive acquaintance with the books; for incidentally, Elseviers printed on papers of varying quality, and sometimes on blue, yellow, or green paper; but even if his opinion were an echo of others, the quotation indicates the printers' good reputation was still current.

There were always those who disagreed with majority opinion, those who thought small Elseviers had scant merit typographically, and the rage for them ridiculous. The types were frequently said to be too condensed. Tannegui Le Febure, concerning the Ovid of Nicolaas Heinsius, remarked, 'I am sorry from the bottom of my heart that the Elseviers in issuing such a work should have neglected the quality of the paper and the printing.' In 1699 in his *Entretiens sur les contes de fées* ..., the Abbé de Villiers gently ridiculed the vogue for Elsevier collecting. He has one of his characters remark:

You know how for a long time the impressions of the Elseviers have been much sought after, even in the country, and I know a man who refuses himself the most necessary things in order to amass, in a library which is empty enough of other books, as many of the little Elseviers as he is able to find. He could reconcile himself to starving in order to have the pleasure of saying, 'I have ten examples of each, and I have them all with the red letters and the right date.'

Some eleven years later Joseph Addison, in his *Spectator*, drew to the life the ridiculous bibliophile whom he christened Tom Folio. Tom was one who had 'greater esteem for *Aldus* and *Elzevir*, than for *Virgil* and *Horace*;' and was of the opinion Horace should be read in the Daniël Heinsius (Elsevier) edition since 'after the strictest and most malicious examination' Tom could find but two faults in him: 'One of them is in the *Aeneid*, where there are two comma's instead of a Parenthesis; and another in the third *Georgick*, where you find a Semicolon turned upside down.'

But despite the few who saw scant virtue in the books their vogue held until the first quarter of the nineteenth century. About that time a decline became perceptible, a waning faced with commendable fortitude by the enthusiastic bibliophile, Mr Thomas Dibdin. Apropros of those decayed times he asks, 'What care I for the capriciousness of public taste? Shall my first folio Aldine Demosthenes and Rhetores be less coveted, less embraced than heretofore?

'Dear as the ruddy drops that warm my heart'

Shall be, to me, my Elzevir and Olivet Ciceros!' Elsewhere he soberly recognized the facts of the case. 'Even in Great Britain and on the Continent,' he observes, 'where scholars have been more conservative in adopting new ideas of education, it is plainly evident that, except in the case of the rarest editions, interest in the classics, as represented by the early editions, Aldines, Elzevirs and the like, has waned very appreciably.' The decline in Elsevier popularity was slowed, in a way, in the later nineteenth century by romantic writers who have the impression that Elseviers are splendid things, even if they don't know exactly why. The attitude is noted by Andrew Lang in his essay on the printers. He remarks that 'You read in novels about 'priceless little Elzevirs,' about books 'as rare as an old Elzevir.' 'I have met,' he says, 'in the works of a lady novelist (but not elsewhere), with an Elzevir Theocritus. The late Mr Hepworth Dixon introduced into one of his romances a romantic Elzevir Greek Testament worth its weight in gold.' Sentimental talk of Elseviers such as Lang cites the reader may himself observe in nineteenth-century literature. When Scott wishes to present an antiquary with all typical trappings it is almost inevitable he should say that Mr Oldbuck's 'little Elzevirs' were the 'trophies of many a walk by night and morning through the Cow- gate, the Canongate, the Bow, Saint Mary's Wynd,— wherever, in fine, there were to be found brokers and trokers, those miscellaneous dealers in things rare and curious.'

Whittier, speaking of his friend, Field, says that

> 'The old, dead authors thronged him round about,
> And Elzevir's gray ghosts from leathern graves looked out.'

In the latter part of the last century, even when biblio- philes speak of Elseviers, there is a counterfeit ring to the enthusiasm. In his *In the Track of the Book-Worm*, Irving Browne asks, 'What reader would not prefer a dainty little Elzevir?' It must have been obvious even then that many, if not most, readers would prefer not to read an Elsevier, and 'dainty' is not the *mot juste* to describe the books. Eugene Field avowed 'It makes me groan to think of the number of Elzevirs that are lost in the libraries of rich parvenus who know nothing of and care nothing for the treasures about them further than a certain vulgar vanity which is involved.' In Field's day, as in our own, although some Elseviers were rare, many were not, and except for literary effect there was no need to reach for smelling salts simply because copies were not all in the hands of the elite.

In twentieth-century America even sentimental regard for the books has largely disappeared. They have been damned rather generally by Daniel B. Updike in his history of printing types. Of the small Elsevier editions of classics Updike observes that 'These editions *were* all very much alike . . . To have seen one Elzevir volume in prose and another in poetry, in this *format*, is to have seen all— or certainly as many as one wishes to see! How anyone ever read with comfort pages so solidly set in such monotonous old style type passes understanding—or at least mine.' He adds the Elseviers employed shortened descenders, 'one reason,' he says, 'why the Elzevir books as reading editions are now failures.'

To a degree, loss of interest in classics resulted in Elseviers losing favor with bibliophiles as well as scholars, since many characteristics of their typography to be appreciated called for knowledge of antiquity. Chapter headings and opening pages, beginning so often with imposing inscriptions set in Roman capitals, were reminiscent to those who had seen classic Roman inscriptions; the device conveyed nothing to those who had not.

Shortened descenders may have made their pages more pleasing to those accustomed to pages of Latin where fewer descenders mar the regularity of type lines; to later ages, shortened letters are merely deformities. The fleuron, which later generations have identified as a buffalo head, was in reality the head of an aegipan. Decorative scrolls surrounded with flowers and birds are obviously derived from Greek and Roman sources. Sirens and masks were conventional classic decorative figures. The mark of Isaac Elsevier, a grapevine entwined about an elm, was borrowed from antiquity, as was the sheaf of arrows and the eagle; and Minerva was the mark of the Amsterdam house. The engraved title-pages had also, of course, meaning and interest for those familiar with classic texts. Knowledge of antiquity was necessary to appreciate Elsevier typography as well as texts. The volumes lost popularity when bibliophiles and readers no longer possessed it.

It should be noted the reputation of the Elseviers did not everywhere decline as rapidly as has been indicated here. Willems, Berghman, and Rahir, who loved the volumes and read the texts, issued their works on the printers in the latter part of the last century, and today on the continent, especially in Holland, Elseviers are current coin; people buy them because they are small, handy editions of texts which they desire. There is also a limited number of people still interested in the Elseviers as printers. Continuing use of their books and interest in their story is a tribute to them which they well deserve, for none can deny these servants and traders in the world of learning left it somewhat better off than they found it, and no denizen of that world can ask for more.

Bibliographical Note

THE great book on the history of the Elseviers is, of course, Alphonse Willems, *Les Elzeviers, Histoire et annales typographiques* ... (Brussels, 1880). It has been used more than any other work in the preparation of this volume. A fairly large literature on the Elseviers existed before Willems' book was published. A bibliographical essay on that literature is contained in the introduction to Willems and needs no repetition here. Willems did considerable original research, but his task was also to a large extent one of verifying, amplifying, and using material gathered by his predecessors. Especially useful to him was W. I. C. R. Elsevier's *Uitkomsten van een onderzoek omtrent de Elseviers, meer bepaaldelijk met opzigt tot derzelver genealogie,* (Utrecht, 1845). Since the appearance of Willems' work a number of important contributions to Elsevier history have appeared. In 1913–24 P. C. Molhuysen published in the series Rijks Geschiedkundige Publicatiën the *Bronnen tot de Geschiedenis der Leidsche Universiteit* in which are to be found not only the proceedings of the academic senate and of the curators and burgomasters in which printing and publishing were frequently discussed, but also many documents concerning the relations of the Elseviers with the University. For the activities of the Elseviers at Amsterdam the most important single source is the documents and letters contained in M. M. Kleerkooper and W. P. van Stockum *De Boekhandel te Amsterdam voornamelijk in de 17e Eeuw, Biographische en Geschiedkundige Aanteekeningen,* (The Hague, 1914–6). Documents concerning the Elsevier shop in the Groote Zaal in the Binnenhof at The Hague are contained in E. F. Kossmann's *De Boekverkoopers, Notarissen en Cramers op het Binnenhof,* (The Hague, 1932).

There have been shorter articles almost without number on the printers, some of them quite valuable. Charles Dumercy threw new light on Louis Elsevier's wanderings before settling at Leyden in his article, 'Louis Elzevier à Anvers et à Liège' (*De Gulden Passer*, Jg. I, 1923). In an article entitled 'Lodewijk Elzevier's geboortejaar' (*Tijdschrift voor boek- en bibliotheekwezen*, Jg. VI, 1908) Alphonse Willems corrected Elsevier chronology as he had previously given it in his book. Valuable documents for the Elseviers at Utrecht were printed by G. A. Evers, 'Joost Elzevier te Utrecht, Pieter Elzevier te Utrecht' in *Het Boek*, V, 1916, and important material on Isaac and Jacob Elsevier at Rotterdam was published by P. Haverkorn van Rijsewijk, 'Bijdrage tot de Geschiedenis der Elseviers' (*Oud Holland*, Jg. XIV, 1896).

In addition to the basic materials listed here, quite a number of letters written by various members of the Elsevier family have been published from time to time, many of them being noted in the catalogue of letters at the University of Leyden Library. Some unpublished letters are also to be found in libraries in the Netherlands. In sketching the historical background, well-known works have been drawn upon, as will be obvious to the historian.

Regarding the bibliography of the Elsevier press, the basic books are first of all that by Alphonse Willems with the two supplementary studies by Gustaf S. Berghman, *Études sur la bibliographie Elzevirienne, basées sur l'ouvrage Les Elzevier de M. Alphonse Willems* (1885), and *Nouvelles études sur la bibliographie Elzevirienne* (1897); and Harold B. Copinger, *The Elzevier Press* ... (1927).